Adventures in Eating :

A Guide to Denver's Ethnic Markets, Bakeries and Gourmet Stores

BY
SUSAN PERMUT

Printed in the United States of America

First Edition
ISBN 0-9638153-1-8

Cover design by Skip Koebbeman
Photography by Shana Vandersluis and Susan Permut
Book design by Skip Koebbeman

Contents

The Adventure Begins

The Adventure Begins...

A ll animals eat to live, but only human beings dine. From a romantic dinner for two to a feast celebrating a birth or a marriage, food is an integral part of the important happenings in our lives. All over the world, people celebrate the special events of their lives and the holidays of their culture with food. We can learn a lot about a nation by learning about what kinds of food they eat. In Denver, we're fortunate in that over the past few years we've seen our city grow, not only in size but in the kinds of people who live here. We've seen the growth of ethnic neighborhoods and ethnic cultures and been enriched by the multiplicity of different kinds of food that are available to us.

This book was written to help you find your way around the wonderfully various and interesting specialty markets in Denver. I've tried to put these markets into categories that make sense, but sometimes it wasn't easy. Many delis also make their own sausage, gourmet markets sometimes include their own coffee bars, bakeries also make wonderful chocolates and so on. It was especially difficult to distinguish between delis and markets, but I finally decided to divide them up rather than have one huge deli/market category, simply because it makes the sections easier to read.

I've listed hours and days that places are open, but please call before you go. Many of these markets are sole proprietorships or mom-and-pop stores, so changes in the family, the season or the marketplace may cause temporary or permanent changes in hours that no-one could have foreseen.

Keep in mind that many items are seasonal, and so even though they were available when I visited the stores, they might not be when you visit. This guide gives just a general idea of the kinds of things carried by each store, so that you can discover other products and ingredients for yourself.

I owe a debt of thanks to all the shopkeepers, bakers, sausagemakers, coffee brewers, chocolatiers and cake decorators who took the time to talk to me, to explain things to me when I didn't understand, to tell me about their food, their businesses and their lives. Almost without exception, I was treated with graciousness and kindness wherever I went. I feel that it has greatly enriched my life and my understanding of people and their cultures to talk to all these entrepreneurs. It's been a wonderful adventure, and I've enjoyed every minute of it.

This is by no means an exhaustive study. I didn't even attempt to include Boulder or other outlying areas, but I hope to do so in the next edition of this book. Even within the Denver area, there are plenty of stores, delis and bakeries I missed this time around, and more are opening up all the time. I describe my visits to you, and give my own impressions and tell you what I think are the best points of each place I go to. This doesn't mean that your impressions will be the same as mine—or even close! Please feel free to write and tell me how you feel about these places, and how your visits differed from mine. Also, please let me know about the places I missed that you have discovered, so I can enjoy them as well. I welcome all comments, criticisms (non-abusive!) and recipes. Write to me care of The Garlic Press at P.O. Box 38163, Denver, Colorado 80238.

If you like to eat, if you're interested in finding out about foods that are unusual and exciting, if you see life as an adventure and would like to participate a little in the cultures and eating habits of others, this book is for you. The adventure continues...

About Denver's Bakeries...

A loaf of bread, a jug of wine and thou...

Edward Fitzgerald,
the Rubaiyat of Omar Khayyam

To me, a fresh loaf of crusty bread, still warm from the oven, is one of the best treats in life. For Europeans, bread is a staple, something to eat with cheese or sausage, something to sop up your soup with, to break off in hunks and devour with fresh butter or olive oil or slice thin with cucumber and serve with tea in china cups.

Who would have known that Denver had such a variety of bakeries? I would never have believed that I would be able to find German bakeries, with delicious tortes and rye breads, a Greek bakery with exotic baklava and galatoboureko, French bakeries displaying baguettes, croissants and brioches, Italian bakeries, full of biscotti and farfalletti, Mexican bakeries, resplendent with conchas, sweet flautas, bolillos and tortillas, and American bakeries, with their pies, pound cakes, lemon bars and brownies.

There's something about fresh bread that satisfies the pangs of hunger and soothes the savage breast better than anything else –and if you're not satisfied with just bread, well, there are those wonderful pastries, muffins, tarts, tortes, and cakes as well!

American Bakeries

Bluepoint Bakery

1307 E. 6th Avenue 839-1820
Monday–Saturday, 7 am–7 pm. Closed Sunday.

The Bluepoint is the blue-blood of American bakeries. And, like a true aristocrat, it's a cut above the rest, looking and tasting simply marvellous, but always basically unassuming, as though unwilling to show the rest of us up as less than perfect.

Breads are available in both plain and fancy here, from olive oil braids to lemon basil campagne. Their pies and tortes are a feast for the eyes, including such delights as strawberry apricot pie and mocha torte. There are fruit-topped cheese florentines, almond cakes dipped in dark chocolate, lemon bars and fabulous citron tarts filled with lemon curd. Take my word for it, the citron tarts are truly heavenly–sweet and creamy but with a hint of tartness–sigh!

Cookies include blackberry thumb prints, pistachio curry cookies (don't worry, the curry taste is intriguing rather than overpowering!) and shortbread for only 35¢ a piece–what a steal!

Offerings vary with the seasons and the baker's whims. But you get an idea of the kind of great treats that await you at the Bluepoint.

Bobby Dazzler

4628 E. 23rd Avenue (23rd & Dexter) 320-4353
Tuesday–Friday, 7am–7pm; Saturday, 7am–4pm.
Closed Sunday & Monday.

Bobby Dazzler is a phrase used in Australia for anything that's terrific, fantastic, incredible. And some of the breads and pastries at this small neighborhood bakery are exactly that! Take, for example, their brioche with cream cheese and strawberries–it's fabulous. Their scones and other specialty breads are equally delicious.

The bakery is run by Amy and Kate. Amy makes the cakes and pies, while Kate handles the breads. Amy explains that they don't make any French pastries or French breads. "We want to be an American-style bakery," she says. "If anything, Kate's influences are Italian. We like to make crusty, rustic breads, fresh fruit pies in season, custard pies, and cakes based on the traditional pound cake."

Since ordinary bread is easy to find, they concentrate on specialty breads that can't be bought at the supermarket, like sourdough Italian and whole wheat Irish soda bread with rosemary, walnuts and garlic, one or two different rye breads a week, a filled bread based on a focaccia dough spread with herbs, salt and olive oil and their very popular bread sticks.

Amy makes most of her cakes as bundt cakes, although they can also be ordered as layer cakes. For example, her favorite kind of wedding cake is lemon pound cake with white pepper and ginger, decorated with fresh flowers and ribbons rather than weighed down with acres of icing. She also makes an orange rum walnut pound cake.

This is a wonderful bakery, with a helpful bunch of people selling delightful baked goods. The collection of rolling pins on the wall is fun, and the changing exhibit in the window reflects the season (Valentine's Day or Christmas) or the inspiration of the owners (four and twenty blackbirds baked in a pie).

Cakes by Karen

6487 Leetsdale 355-1300; 8100 W. Crestline, Littleton 972-4779;
7562 S. University Blvd, Littleton 779-0825; 1475 Kipling, Lakewood
234-1919; 15433 E. Hampden, Aurora 693-7454
10691 Melody Dr, Northglenn 452-6801
Monday–Friday, 9 am–6 pm; Saturday, 9 am–5 pm.
Closed Sunday.

Cakes by Karen is almost exclusively cakes for special occasions that need to be ordered in advance. The only location where you can get cakes to go is in Northglenn. They have a variety of cakes, which can be ordered just a day in advance, and they have several books for you to look through and steal some ideas.

The thing I like best about Karen's is their fun, unusually shaped cakes, like the one shaped like a tombstone, inscribed, "We mourn the passing of your youth". They have rattle-shaped cakes for baby showers, Barbie doll cakes, where the cake is actually the skirt of the Barbie doll, and a radio-shaped cake for teens that is very fun and silly.

There's also a book of X-rated cakes that are, surprisingly, almost as risqué as those from Le Bakery Sensual. But my favorite was the pizza cake. It looks just like a pizza, but it's cake. That's Italian!

BREAD PUDDING

This is my favorite bread pudding recipe. Served in a small pool of lemon sauce with a mound of whipped cream on top, it's food for the gods!

1 cup milk
4 cups bread, cubed
3 eggs
1 cup sugar
1-1/2 teaspoons vanilla
Grated rind and juice of 1 lemon
Grated rind and juice of 1 orange

Pour milk over cubed bread in baking dish. Beat eggs and add sugar, vanilla, rinds and juices. Let sit until bread is thoroughly soaked. Bake in 350° oven for about 45 minutes. Serve with lemon sauce and whipped cream.

LEMON SAUCE

Juice from 2 lemons
2 tablespoons grated lemon rind
1/3 cup sugar (or more, to taste)
2/3 cup water, divided
1 teaspoon vanilla
1 tablespoon cornstarch

Squeeze lemon juice into saucepan with sugar, rind and 1/3 cup of water. Stir till sugar is dissolved. Dissolve cornstarch in 1/3 cup of water. Add to mixture in saucepan and cook until it begins to boil and thickens slightly. Add vanilla essence. Serve with bread pudding.

Whipped cream on top completes the decadence!

Child's Pastry Garden

Monaco & Yale 757-1285
Tuesday–Friday, 7 am–6:30 pm; Saturday, 8 am–6 pm;
Sunday, 10 am–3 pm; Monday, 8 am–6:30 pm.
Child's Pastry Shop
311 E. County Line, Littleton 347-0246
Tuesday–Saturday, 8 am–6 pm; Sunday, 10 am–3 pm;
Monday, 10 am–6 pm.

The first thing anyone who's lived in Denver for a while will tell you is that Child's specializes in special occasion cakes: birthdays, weddings or other events allow Child's to exercise their special expertise and create something unique especially for you. In fact, visiting the new store on Monaco and Yale, the first thing I notice when I walk in the door is the wedding consultant, sitting right up front ready to help any blushing or not-so-blushing bride who walks in.

Of course they're also a full-service bakery, with many different kinds of bread, dinner rolls, croissants and a large variety of pies and cakes. I see a beautiful carrot cake decorated with little frosted carrots. It's charming. Their strawberry pies and other fruit pies are attractive looking, as are their cream pies and German chocolate brownies. They have pound cakes, lemon roll cakes, brownies and many others. I know people who won't go anywhere else for their birthday cakes.

Fratelli's

1200 E. Hampden, Englewood (Old Hampden at Downing) 761-4771
Monday–Thursday, 6:30 am–10:30 pm; Friday & Saturday till 11;
Sunday, 6:30 am–9 pm.

Fratelli's is actually an Italian restaurant, but they have such an extensive array of baked goods that it seems necessary to include them! For example, they make over 300 lbs. of fresh breadsticks every day for the restaurant and bakery, in several different flavors, all delicious. They have fresh danish, cinnamon rolls, caramel

and pecan rolls, cheesecakes with fresh fruit, several varieties of fresh bread each day and daily special sweet breads, of which my favorite is lemon bread. This is like a cross between a pound cake and a sweet bread, with the sharpness of lemon and a sweet sugar glaze.

Jim Plummer, owner of Fratelli's, makes his own fresh pasta for sale, as well. Lemon pepper, tomato, verde (eggless spinach pasta), whole wheat and egg pasta are available every day. While you're there, you might want to pick up one or two of their cannolis, because they're really good. You can also buy lasagne and other Italian delights in large quantities for parties.

Great Harvest Bread Company

765 S. Colorado Boulevard (Belcaro Shopping Center) 778-8877
Monday–Friday, 6 am–7 pm; Sunday, 6 am–6 pm.
Also: 80th & Wadsworth, Arvada 420-0500
South University & Orchard (Cherry Hills Marketplace) 347-8767

How wonderful to walk into any one of these three locations and be offered a slice of fresh bread to taste! All their bread is made from 100% organic wheat milled daily at each of their stores. They have honey whole wheat, sunflower whole wheat, light wheat and white, as well as many specialty breads like oat poppy seed, date nut spice, jalapeño corn bread, orange pecan, tomato basil and others too numerous to mention! Not all specialty breads are always available, but they welcome orders.

They also have several variations on cinnamon rolls here and several kinds of bread sticks. They give out a Bread Owner's Manual that explains how to care for and enjoy your fresh, delicious bread. The manual even tells you how to slice your own bread, since the Great Harvest feels (and I defi-nitely agree with them!) that bread is fresher and better if you slice it yourself instead of having them slice it for you. They will slice most varieties if you really want them to, however!

I just love walking in and being offered a slice of their bread. And they offer children their choice of bread sticks. An organic hurrah to Great Harvest for their nice attitude and their good, wholesome bread!

Manna Bakery

1500 W. Littleton Boulevard, Littleton 798-7117
Monday–Friday, 7 am–6 pm; Saturday, 7:30 am–5 pm. Closed Sunday.

This bakery also offers catering and sandwiches. They have a large variety of muffins: apple oat bran, banana nut, banana chocolate chip, mandarin orange, carrot walnut, peach bran and poppy seed, to mention a few. I particularly like the poppy seed. They have cream and fruit pies, and specialty cakes like carrot cake, strudel, coffee cakes, baklava, éclairs and brownies. Breads include white, seven grain, honey whole wheat, German black rye and sourdough. They make cakes for special occasions, including wedding cakes. On their brochure is the plea,

PLEASE...Place cake orders 48 hours ahead of time. Miracles, although rare, can sometimes happen on shorter notice.

I appreciate the attitude of the Manna Bakery in acknowledging that we all sometimes leave things till the last minute. It's nice to know they're still willing to try to accommodate us.

Vollmers Bakery

1331 E. Colfax 832-8830
Monday–Saturday, 6:30 am–6:30 pm. Closed Sunday.

Vollmers has breads of all descriptions, from raisin, cinnamon and other sweet breads to whole wheat, pumpernickel, sourdough, egg bread and white. They have croissants and cookies, pies, coffee cakes and fruit stollen. Tortes are also available, from their six layer lemon torte, which is one of their most popular, to German chocolate, French vanilla or Grand Marnier. Their large variety of cheesecakes includes lemon, turtle and caramel pecan.

The poppy seed log is one of their most popular items. It has a rich poppy seed filling in a soft, sweet dough. This is a spacious, attractive bakery with a friendly, helpful staff.

Warren Paul's Grand Central Station

2015 E. 17th Avenue 399-5181
Monday–Friday, 11:30 am–6:30 pm; Saturday, noon–5 pm. Closed Sunday.

Warren Paul is a man who's passionate about pastrami, keen on knishes, and has a lust for lox. He orders the best pastrami and slices it just right, the leanest, tastiest corned beef and his lox is the highest quality from New York. He makes chicken and beef pot pies, eggplant lasagne, eggplant parmesan hero sandwiches ("Very popular in New York") and has gourmet takeout to make your home dining easier without being lower in quality–and you never even have to dirty a dish!

This joint used to be known as "Cheesecakes and More" and Warren cranks out a mean cheesecake, as well as making his own seasonal fruit pies, a chocolate mousse cake that's excellent and other baked goods as diverse as scones and rugalach. Sometimes Warren's so busy in the kitchen it looks a little like the bomb hit up front, but the food is always delicious.

Wheat Ridge Dairy & Bakery

8000 W. 44th Avenue, Wheat Ridge 424-5151
Monday–Saturday, 6 am–8 pm; Sunday, 8 am–4 pm.

From the outside, this place looks like a big old barn that's about to fall down any minute. In fact, cows chewed the cud outside just thirty years ago! Inside, it's a bakery and restaurant reminiscent of the 50's. The bakery case is filled with pies topped with whipped cream, pastries and enormous danishes. They have ice cream as well. They're particularly proud of their special occasion cakes, but for me the kick is the quick trip back in time as you walk through the door!

Asian Bakeries

Celestial Bakery

333 S. Federal (in the Far East Center) 936-2339
Daily, 10 am–7 pm. Closed Wednesday.

This bakery bills itself as the sole authentic Asian bakery this side of the Mississippi! They have egg custard pies, red bean filled buns, coconut cream buns, and a wonderful tofu pudding, with a sweet topping. This pudding is rather like an Asian version of flan. (In many Asian countries, they don't routinely drink milk or use milk products, so soy products or coconut milk take the place of these in their diet. In fact, for many Asians, even the smell of cheese is quite repulsive, and they avoid it.) Celestial Bakery sells some savory pastries as well as a number of side dishes, including sticky rice and other rice dishes. French-style layer cakes are sold by the slice.

Forever Bakery

1008 S. Federal Boulevard 922-2446
Daily, 10 am–7 pm. Closed Tuesday.

This bakery wasn't open when I was first researching this book, but there were several wedding cakes in the window, and the sign said they would be selling bridal cakes, French pastries and vegetarian products. Khanh (or Connie) and her mother were inside, busily trying to get things ready for the opening.

They were so friendly and nice, I wanted to come back and see if they were open–and they are! The shop is owned by Quan Le and his wife Huong. She's the one who makes the gorgeous French pastries, like éclairs, fruit tarts, and rum babas, and she designs and makes the beautifully decorated wedding cakes. She learned how to do this in Vietnam. The whole family is vegetarian so they have a variety of vegetarian meats for sale in the refrigerator case, as well as bicuon chay, a Vietnamese appetizer of eggroll skins filled with tofu. They also serve croissant sandwiches.

Quan and Huong Le left Vietnam with their two daughters during the fall of Saigon. "We didn't even have shoes," Quan says.

Korean Rice Cake O Bok Teok

9830 E. Colfax, Aurora 367-8989
Tuesday–Saturday, 10:30 am–6 pm. Closed Sunday & Monday.

This very small but cute bakery is owned by Grace and Tom Min. Grace tries to explain to me what they have in the bakery case, but it's tough going, because although her English sounds very good, it's limited in scope. There are several kinds of large sweet rice cakes, which could be cut into pieces for serving and some round Japanese-style small rice cakes.

When I return later, her husband, Tom, is here. He's anxious to explain to me what everything is, and how it can be used. All the bakery and noodle-type products are made of rice and sweet rice. Rice cakes with yellow beans can be used for main dishes or desserts. There are also cooked cylinders of rice that can be sliced and served with a hot and spicy pepper sauce or cooked in soup.

I buy a cake made of sweet rice, pinon nuts, sugar and raisins that's very popular with our dinner guests.

Vinh Xuong Bakery

375 S. Federal Boulevard (in the Far East Center) 922-4968
Daily, 9:30 am – 8:30 pm.

Two doors down from the Thai Bin Duong market in the Far East Center, Vinh Xuong is a delightful little bakery, where they have the largest almond cookies I've ever seen. They also have small almond cookies that are similar to shortbread, and two kinds of what I can only describe as Oriental doughnuts. The round ones are covered with sesame seeds and filled with sweet yellow bean curd or–my favorite–coconut. The flat ones are plain. I also try a large, lemon-flavored cupcake that is quite delicious. They have other desserts, like sweet rice, tapioca, and several other desserts made with coconut milk. They serve steamed dim sum-like dumplings for breakfast!

The lady behind the counter is very helpful and manages to communicate with me, even though she speaks no English and I speak no Asian languages! She wants to be sure I'll tell my readers that her bakery goods are delicious and very well priced. If you're interested in sampling some out-of-the-ordinary baked goods, explore the possibilities at Vinh Xuong.

Bagel Bakeries

The Bagel Nook Bakery

6480 Wadsworth, Arvada 431-6311
Monday–Friday, 6 am–6 pm; Saturday, 6 am–5 pm. Closed Sunday.

The Bagel Nook South
7175 W. Jefferson, Lakewood 988-5926
Monday–Thursday, 7:30 am–3:30 pm; Friday, 7:30 am–3 pm.
Closed Saturday & Sunday.

For seven years, the Bagel Nook has been pleasing customers in Arvada with a variety of bagels: plain, onion, sesame, poppy seed, wheat, garlic, pumpernickel, cinnamon raisin, egg, blueberry and sunflower–and an equally large variety of spreads: whipped butter, honey butter, cream cheese, cream cheese with chives, strawberry cream cheese, garden vegetable, wildberry... you get the picture.

They also have sandwiches, a pizza bagel, cakes, pies, brownies, and an item called the Nooky, which is a wiener wrapped in egg bagel dough, topped with cheese and baked. This is a pleasant place with a cheerful staff. So if you're looking for a little Nooky, or just a bagel or pie or a sandwich, you'll probably find it at the Bagel Nook, or even at the Bagel Nook South!

The Bagel Stop

2412 E. Arapahoe, Littleton 220-5101
Monday–Friday, 6 am–6 pm; Saturday & Sunday, 6 am–3 pm.

The Bagel Stop is small but friendly, and has some interesting variations on the usual litany of bagels. For example, how about a Bulldog– a kosher frankfurter baked in bagel dough? Or a Pizzabagel –pizza sauce and mozzarella on half a bagel? They also have the more usual Lox-a-Bagel–basically a bagel sandwich of lox, cream cheese, tomato and

onion. They do have regular bagels, like honey wheat, salt, herb and pumpernickel–but then they also have egg jalapeño and fresco, as well. Fresco is a honey wheat bagel rolled in cinnamon and sugar–closest thing to it would be a cinnamon roll!

The Bagel Stop also has several different flavors of whipped cream cheese: strawberry, lox, honey walnut raisin and chives, among others. One very nice thing they do offer is a baker's half-dozen: one bagel free with each half dozen, instead of the usual baker's dozen. They have sandwiches and drinks as well. Next time you find yourself torn between Jewish and Italian food, stop in for a Pizzabagel!

The Bagel Store

942 S. Monaco 388-2648
Monday–Friday, 6 am–6 pm; Saturday & Sunday, 6 am–5 pm.

This little store has been in business for 14 years, making bagels of all varieties: pumpernickel, rye, whole wheat, onion, garlic, poppyseed,

rye, cinnamon and raisin...

They also make a variety of breads, like challah, pumpernickel, wheat and rye. Their cakes include banana nut cake, honeycake with raisins and poppyseed cake. This is a kosher bakery, which is quite unusual these days.

Dave–Pan Bagel Bakery

1907 S. Havana, Aurora 745-1154
Monday–Friday , 6:30 am–4:30 pm;
Saturday & Sunday, 8:30 am–4:30 pm.

Yes, they have bagels! Any kind you could possibly imagine, almost, including egg, chocolate chip, raisin bran, garlic, onion, whole wheat, poppy, sesame, five grain... They also sell deli sandwiches, including all kinds of bagel sandwiches and have their own homemade chocolate chip cookies. Some of their sandwich names are quite original–can you imagine what a hot cow might be? Does it bring to mind hot pastrami, lettuce, tomato and Dijon mustard?

Dave makes all his bagels fresh daily and also has bagel chips. These could develop into a major addiction. Try them and you'll see what I mean.

Jacobs Bagelry

290 S. Downing 744-6028
Monday–Friday, 6:30 am–3 pm; Saturday, 7:30 am–3 pm;
Sunday, 8 am–3 pm.

Homemade bagels are really good. Combine them with gourmet coffees like lattes and cappuccinos and you have a wonderful combination. Jacob's has a large variety of bagels, like onion, garlic, poppy and sesame seed, as well as blueberry and bran muffins, and flavored cream cheeses to spread on them, like herb and spice, strawberry and walnut raisin. They serve breakfast, which includes offerings like eggs with ham or sausage, and lunch, with sandwiches like turkey, chicken breast and BLT's. This is an island of calm created at a busy intersection, run by an exceptionally helpful group of people.

New York Bagel Boys

6449 E. Hampden (Hampden and Monaco) 759-2212
Tuesday–Saturday, 7 am–6:30 pm; Sunday, 7 am–4:30 pm.

The smell of fresh bagels when you walk into this great little bagelry makes it just like walking into an old-fashioned bakery. Perhaps most bakeries don't bake during the day anymore, so that great crusty smell doesn't always hit you, but at the New York Bagel Boys I've often been in when they're pulling the bagels out of the oven and the smell is heavenly!

The range of available bagel flavors is pretty amazing: from garlic, onion and pumpernickel to raisin and, on occasion, blueberry, and everything imaginable in between. They're all good, though I have a special fondness for egg bagels and whole wheat myself. The New York Bagel Boys also has fresh challah (Jewish egg bread), braided or regular loaves, with poppyseeds or sesame seeds, bialys, Jewish rye and some cookies and pastries.

If you happen to go in around Purim (the Jewish holiday celebrating the victory of Queen Esther and the Jewish people over the evil villain Haman) you might get to taste a real treat: hamantaschen. Supposedly shaped like the evil Haman's hat, these are pastries filled with poppyseed and dates. They also have other seasonal delights. This is my favorite place for bagels and egg bread.

Danish Bakeries

Danish Delight Bakery

7475 East Arapahoe Road, Englewood 771-3314
Monday, 6:30 am–noon; Tuesday–Friday, 6:30 am–6:30 pm;
Saturday, 6:30 am–5 pm. Closed Sunday.

This Danish bakery is owned by Erick Kristensen, who does all the baking. His specialty is homemade cheese kringles, which are ring-shaped butter layered pastries, quite large, with marzipan, custard and raisins. The dough is flavored with cardamom.These are a Danish Christmas specialty (Kris Kringle is Santa Claus in the Scandinavian countries) but at Danish Delight they're available year-round.

Erick bakes a variety of Scandinavian and northern European specialties, including Danish butter cookies, strudels (raspberry, blueberry, peach, cherry, and apricot), Danish pastries of course, rum balls with raspberries, rugalach, both regular and miniature, Sacher tortes, fruit and cream pies, Black Forest cake and delicate cream puffs.

His breads include rye, cinnamon, challah (Jewish egg bread) and Swiss farms bread, which is half rye and half white. There are rolls and enormous bran muffins. Danish macaroons, fruit slices and even baklava are there to tempt the palate. Erick's recipes are from the old world. And, like most bakeries, he's willing to make custom cakes for weddings and parties. This place is a little gem, authentic and friendly, with a large variety of different baked goods. Everything is made with butter, and from scratch. You could probably put on weight just breathing the air in here–but it would be worth it.

Eastern European Bakeries

Mama Pirogi's & Other Peasantries

2033 E. 13th Avenue 320-5608
Wednesday–Sunday, 7 am–6 pm; Monday & Tuesday, 7 am–noon.

So–what is a pirogi, anyway? Well, it's the same as a piroshki (that helps, doesn't it?) –a turnover filled with meat, vegetables and/or potatoes. This bakery has lots of great peasant breads and desserts, but nary a pirogi that I could find. Talking to Walter, the owner, I find out that that's because he usually makes them in the winter, when the north wind doth blow and we all crave something to stick to our ribs! Mama Pirogi's is definitely worth a visit, because of all the unusual taste treats you can enjoy here. Many are made from old family recipes, and all are traditional–not low-fat or low-sugar.

Mama Pirogi's has a few tables where you can sit and sample a Russian tea cake or raspberry rugalach, or perhaps a lemon bar or some mandelbrot. They make kolache here, a Czech peasant bread from Eastern Europe,

made with honey and poppy-seed filling. They claim to have the best carrot cake in the world. A 2 layer cake weighs 10 lbs.–that means a lot of carrots gave their lives! Their Ukrainian poppyseed cake and toffee bars are equally well-loved. Walter also makes a breakfast pastry called schnecken, filled with poppyseeds and figs.

This is probably the best Eastern European bakery in town–but then it's also the only Eastern European bakery in town.

French Bakeries

Chateau de Patisserie Bakery and Cafe

7400 E. Hampden (Tiffany Plaza) 770-9439
Monday–Friday, 6:30 am–6 pm; Saturday, 7 am–6 pm;
Sunday, 8 am–4 pm.

Baked goods, a small cafe and the usual gourmet coffee drinks: cappuccinos, lattes and a special coffee of the day are all available here. The baked goods are similar to those available at La Petite Boulangerie. They have good bread, including baguettes, sourdough bread, egg twists and muffins. Their muffins include lemon poppyseed and blueberry. There are also brownie macaroons, shortbread cookies with frosting, and flavored croissants. Also available are gourmet hot teas and ice cream.

French Confection

300 Fillmore, 399-3811
Monday–Thursday, 7 am–7:30 pm; Friday & Saturday, 7 am–9:30 pm;
Sunday, 9 am–5 pm.

This charming bakery and chocolaterie is one of my favorite places in Cherry Creek to sit outside in the summer, with coffee and a pastry, and watch the world go by. Their pastries are incredibly beautiful, and taste as good as they look. Their fresh fruit tarts, almond cream tortes and coconut orange cheese cakes are fabulous, and their muffins and white chocolate cherry kirsch tartes are no less tasty and delicious.

In summer, they offer strawberry lemonade, and they have the usual selection of gourmet coffee drinks. Their Mont Blanc gourmet hot cocoa is sold in ritzy department stores like Marshall Fields and was even taken by a party that was climbing Everest. They make specialty chocolates and serve coffees, cappuccinos and lattes. The cafe is small but attractive and European-looking, with black and white tile, and the outside seating is equally miniscule. But it's a lovely place to sit and watch the Cherry Creek hoi polloi go by.

La Patisserie Francaise

7885 Wadsworth, Arvada 424-5056
Monday–Friday, 8 am–7 pm; Saturday, 9 am–6 pm. Closed Sunday.

Just walk into this bakery in a shopping center in Arvada and it feels like walking into a French patisserie. They make wonderful baked goods here, all made with lots of butter and sugar, all sinfully delicious and made the old-fashioned way. Meringues, lemon mousse cakes, langues de chat, fresh fruit tarts–everything looks beautiful and wonderfully authentic.

They have gateaux, truffles and other chocolates and something called bustock–a bread pudding. And, of course, you can buy breads, especially French baguettes, here. If you're looking for a French bakery in the northwest part of town, this is it!

La Petite Boulangerie

8 metro area locations, including Larimer Square, Cherry Creek, Arvada, Aurora, Englewood & Arvada.

1884 15th St. (15th & Larimer) 534-4460
Monday–Friday, 6:30 am–6 pm; Saturday, 8 am–4 pm;
Sunday, 8 am–2 pm. (Call other stores for hours and exact locations)

At this bakery, they make everything right in the store, including baguettes and other breads like honey wheat, raisin nut, rye, egg twists and nine grain. Their most unusual items are a variety of flavored croissants, including almond, cheese, apple and even chocolate chip. Bagels range from onion and sesame to chocolate chip to garlic. Their muffins include bran, blueberry, raspberry and chocolate chip and they also have Danish pastries, turnovers and coffee cake.

The bakeries also make sandwiches and have coffee, hot chocolate and soft drinks available.

Presidential Food Facts

Warren Harding's dog, Laddie Boy, had a birthday party with a cake made of layers of dog biscuits topped with icing.

Le Délice

250 Steele 331-0972
Monday, 7 am–6 pm; Tuesday–Saturday, 7 am–9 pm. Closed Sunday.

Billed as a "very French bakery", Le Délice is a very delightful garden level bakery in Cherry Creek. They use no fat or sugar in any of their breads, and everything is made from scratch. The Danish pastries are made with croissant dough, and the fruit mousse cakes and tarts are all made from fresh fruit or fresh fruit purée. Le Délice is owned by Maurice and Nicole Cochard. Maurice spent 11 years as the executive chef at Lafitte's, the very traditional French restaurant that was downtown in Larimer Square for many years.

Their fresh fruit tartes, fresh charlottes, fruit mousse cakes and tartes lunettes–shortbread cookies pressed together with raspberry jam, are quite wonderful. Their boules and baguettes are as beautiful as any that I've seen wobbling in the bicycle baskets of French men and women on their way home from the boulangerie in any little French town or village. They also taste as delicious–crusty, fresh and flavorful.

Surprisingly, Le Délice also has a small but interesting selection of French deli items like rillettes de Tours (a specialty item made of pork, rather like a coarse paté), goose liver mousse, creme fraiche (that wonderful, slightly sour cross between whipped cream and sour cream that's so hard to duplicate in the U.S.) and Camembert, Brie and European-style unsalted butter.

Their chocolate mousse cake is called simply "Le Délice". Try it if you're not afraid of chocolate overload. This is a lovely little bakery that serves meals as well. It's downstairs, at garden level, right next door to the Continental Deli.

Bread Museum

Just outside of Paris there's a Bread Museum, the Musée Français du Pain, with antique bread boards, knives, metal molds, manuscripts and memorabilia dedicated to celebrating the "staff of life". There are signs from old bakeries, miniature replicas of old wood-fired ovens and representations of Saint-Honoré, the patron saint of bakers.

Paris Bakery

1272 S. Sheridan   935-9353
Monday, 8 am – 3 pm; Tuesday – Saturday, 8 am – 5 pm. Closed Sunday.

The first thing you notice when you walk into this immaculate little bakery on South Sheridan is the special cakes created by baker Rinaldo Suel. I'm amazed by a huge hamburger-looking cake sitting next to a cake shaped like a Thanksgiving turkey, cooked and garnished for the table. In another case are a witch's head (on a platter, rather like John the Baptist's!) and a very cute little dog, curled up as though he's in front of the fire on a winter evening. Rinaldo's creations are produced in great detail for special orders, and they're spectacular.

Rinaldo and his wife Anne are both French, and have been running the bakery here together for a year and a half. Their cinnamon rolls are so good that they're working on selling them wholesale. They are lower in sugar and fat than cinnamon rolls usually are. They'll also be selling the batter, which I will be first in line to buy!

The bakery itself has little tables and chairs, so you can sit and have coffee and a pastry if you want. They have fresh-baked bread (of course, it's a bakery!), pies (cherry, peach and apple), cakes and cookies. Their style is more homemade than what we often think of as a French bakery, but everything is good and tasty, with an emphasis on less fat and sugar. The lace curtain in the window and the copper molds on the wall make it a cosy, country French kind of place.

Sweet Soirée

4182 E. Virginia   388-3655   Fax: 399-4641
Monday – Friday, 7:30 am – 5:30 pm; Saturday, 7:30 am – 5 pm.
Closed Sunday.

This French-style bakery is part of Le Petit Gourmet catering, so as well as baked goods of all kinds, they also have soups, nut breads, hors d'oeuvres and quiches to take out and a complete catering and box lunch service as well. The bakery specializes in French pastries and cakes, like Sacher tortes, fruit pies, Black Forest cakes and other mouth-watering sweet things. They also have cookies, meringue cases, breads, croissants, vol au vent cases, strudels and sweet rolls. Specially decorated cakes for weddings, birthdays and other occasions are also available.

Sweet Soirée has a comprehensive brochure with prices that also has descriptions of all their cakes. Some items require prior notice, but their on-site selection is broad enough that you wouldn't be disappointed to just drop in and pick up a dessert or two. Everything is made with butter and cream, a treat for the eye as well as the palate. If you're watching your waistline, beware!

German & Swiss Bakeries

André's Confiserie Suisse

370 S. Garfield 322-8871
Tuesday–Friday, 9 am–5:30 pm; Saturday, 9 am–4 pm.
Closed Sunday & Monday.

The cakes and pastries at André's are superior to those you find in ordinary bakeries. Their little lemon tarts, for example, sweet pastry filled with tart, luscious lemon curd, are a taste explosion in your mouth. Their strawberry kirsch tarts taste like strawberries, not sugar syrup, with light cream and cake. Their tortes are outstanding, and conjure up images of birthday parties for young Victorian ladies, who would sit in their satin dresses and drink tea and eat Black Forest torte or puff pastry Bavarian topped with bavarian cream and fresh fruit, that looks as delectable as it tastes.

Of course, André's is open for morning and afternoon coffee and pastries, but it's hard to imagine having the time to indulge in such luxury. A Swiss friend of mine told me that her mother shopped twice a day, once for the noon meal and once for the evening meal, and each shopping trip was an occasion for cakes and coffee with her friends at a nearby cafe after they'd finished their shopping. These must have been the original kaffee klatsches!

André's also has a small but wonderful selection of chocolates, as well as some Swiss products, like Knorr soups and mixes for making sauces for sauerbraten or beef bourguignon, and Lindt chocolate from Switzerland. You can pick up some Twinings tea, to take home to eat with those spectacular rum babas, chocolate rum balls or napoleons. Their breads are also wonderful: kugelhopf, brioche and croissants, among others.

Das Meyer Fine Pastry Chalet

13251 W. 64th, Arvada 425-5616
Tuesday–Saturday, 7 am–6 pm. Closed Sunday & Monday.

At first this location seems a most unlikely spot for a charming little Victorian-style bakery. However, it's next to Morningside Manor, a wedding reception facility, which is useful for the wedding cake business. Dennis and Elaine Meyer are very concerned about offering the best to their customers, and their care and concern are evident in every detail of Das Meyer.

You enter the bakery/cafe over a romantic little hump-backed bridge. Once inside, there are chintz curtains and a Victorian country atmosphere. They offer wonderful rich German pastries, including strudels, dobisches (tortes with seven layers), cream and fruit pies and great specialty breads, like orange marmalade bread, which is fantastic.

Great cakes, like napoleons, éclairs, lemon bars, several kinds of brownies and butter cookies sit temptingly behind the glass of the cases, begging to be boxed and taken home or eaten right there with tea or coffee.

Dennis has a case of ribbons and trophies for culinary awards–mostly for his wedding cakes. They've been in business since 1982, but in this location only for the last nine months. They work with a lot of caterers and wedding planners and make 15–25 wedding cakes each weekend.

"We have a truly international cake decorating team," says Dennis. "Russian, Romanian, Mexican, Jewish, German and Australian–we have all the options covered."

Dimmers Home Bakery

2832 S. Havana, Aurora 751-8611
Tuesday–Friday, 8 am–6 pm; Saturday 8 am–5 pm. Closed Sunday.

This attractive German bakery has the real smell of a genuine old European bakery. It's unmistakable, and seems to come from only using fresh ingredients and lots of butter, cream and sugar! The cakes and tortes are gorgeous–Black Forest and hazelnut, almond petits fours, éclairs, rum balls and assorted French pastries.

The German specialties include cherry strudel, chocolate marmork, streusel cookies, schweine ohren (pigs' ears–but different from those at the the Rheinlander bakery: here they have a little chocolate on the ends), Linzertorte and bienenkuchen.

The bakery is owned by Dasha Majer and her husband Paul, who make everything with fresh ingredients and no preservatives. They make their own fillings, like the poppyseed filling for the poppyseed roll and the fillings for the raspberry and apricot kuchen. There is also a small selection of boxed chocolates from Germany, Austria and Switzerland. This bakery was in business on the west side of town for 35 years, run by Jakob and Katharina Dimmer (see Rheinlander Bakery, below) and has been in its present location for a little over a year.

If you're looking for authentic German rye bread, they have that too. This is a place that prides itself on its fine, old-country baking.

Rheinlander Bakery

5721 Olde Wadsworth Boulevard, Arvada 467-1810
10354 N. Federal, Federal Heights 469-8572
Monday–Saturday, 6 am–6 pm; Sunday, 8 am–3 pm.

Walking down the street in Arvada's Old Town just as the bells are ringing at noon one spring day, it almost feels like being in Europe! Going into the Rheinlander Bakery makes it seem even more so. They claim to have the most authentic German rye bread in Denver, and offer many old world favorites, like the highest quality coffee cakes and fruit and cheese Danish, schweine ohren (literally 'pigs' ears')–for the shape, fortunately, not the taste!–bienenstich–a German coffee cake with honey and slivered almonds, and Linzer tarts. There are also Russian tea cookies, baklava, and potica, an

Eastern European delight with poppy seeds and walnuts. They also have many tortes, including hazelnut and Bavarian cream.

Their pastries are very good and very rich–all made with butter and the highest quality ingredients. The bakery was established in 1986, a second generation family-owned business. Edward and Maro Dimmer continue the tradition of Edward's parents, Jakob and Katharina Dimmer, who were famous for their rye bread, German tortes and pastries.

They make special cakes for weddings, graduations etc. The old world tradition is continued in their wedding cake brochure, where they say,

Our Gift to You

The servings per wedding cake include the top tier which is traditionally reserved for your first anniversary. Please feel free to serve this tier to your guests and we will duplicate a top tier free of charge on your first anniversary. This is because we believe you should enjoy the cake as it is meant to be, fresh and delicious.

A charming new twist on an old tradition, I think.

A sister store in Federal Heights is supplied from this store, where the main bakery is, so if you're looking for a touch of old Europe, visit the Rheinlander. The service is friendly and knowledgeable, the selection is excellent and the pastries are sinfully rich.

Greek Bakeries

Omonia Bakery

2813 E. Colfax 394-9333
Daily, 9 am–10 pm.

Some people are just a pleasure to talk with, and Dino Karas, owner and baker at this lovely Greek bakery, is one of them. He makes all kinds of bread here–French bread, as well as Easter bread and Christmas bread (which are basically the same and available fresh at Christmas and Easter, frozen during the rest of the year). These holiday breads are made with eggs, milk, and fruit.

His Greek pastries are various and delicious: baklava, kataifi, koulourakia, and galatoburiko. This last is my personal favorite. In Oxford, when I was in high school, I worked for a summer in a little restaurant called The Town and Gown, meaning that it served both the town and the university. It was run by two lovely Greek families from Cyprus, who immediately practically adopted me into their family. When the shipment of Greek pastries arrived in late afternoon once a week, all work in the restaurant stopped abruptly, and the entire family, including me, sat down for coffee and galatoburiko. I must say that Dino's is at least as good as ours was then!

His French-style pastries are also fabulous, especially the apricot-flavored layer cake. His cookies are rich and tasty, and he also makes custom wedding and other special occasion cakes. This bakery has been in the neighborhood for eleven years—the first five across the street where the Ethiopian Restaurant is now and the last six at its present location.

This is a cafe as well as a bakery, so you can stop in for a pastry and coffee almost any time during the day. The atmosphere is relaxed and friendly, just like a small, European cafe. It's a custom in the Greek Orthodox Church for people to take a cake to church for families to share. Families take turns to bring this cake and Dino has standing orders for them every week.

Italian Bakeries

Gaspare's Bakery

3890 Kipling, Wheat Ridge 423-5818
Monday–Saturday, 7 am–7 pm; Sunday, 8 am–3 pm.

The smell of anise is strong as you walk into Gaspare's. The cakes and cookies are all beautifully arranged: biscotti, fig-filled ladyfingers, raspberry farfalletti, tutti frutti cookies edged with chocolate, marzipan cookies that melt in your mouth, and many more, too numerous to mention! Their coffee cakes look like deep dish pies, topped with streusel. Lemon-filled cakes and ricotta-filled crispy shells vie for attention with exquisite cakes topped with fresh fruit, and creamy, rich tiramisu.

Breads include semolina, Sicilian, and traditional Italian.

There's also a deli department, with mozzarella, capocollo, mortadella, olives, cannolis and a good selection of imported pastas. There are tables, so you can sit and enjoy a sandwich or coffee and a pastry if you wish.

Mexican Bakeries

El Alamo Bakery

3165 W. 38th Avenue 477-8114
Daily, 6 am–8 pm.

El Alamo used to be an Italian bakery, but since it was taken over by Hector and Blanca Castillo, the bakery now has both Italian and Mexican baked specialties. They make Mexican sweet bread–small loaves called bolillos–as well as Italian bread, which has always been excellent, with a distinctive taste and crusty exterior.

Pies and cheesecakes are available, as well as Italian rum cake and many varieties of Italian cookies. The Mexican-style cakes they've added are conchas, flaky pastries shaped like horns, polvorones (known to us gringos as Mexican wedding cookies), exponjas and sweet flautas, which have a pineapple or raspberry filling.

There's a rack of Mexican spices, including lavender flowers, sassafras (it makes great tea!), cedar, cascara, star anise and manzanilla (chamomile). I hope they keep both the Italian and the Mexican baked specialties at this bakery. It's a great combination.

La Favorita

2925 W. 38th Avenue 477-9658
Monday–Saturday, 8 am–8 pm. Closed Sunday.

This is a take-out Mexican food place as well as the retail outlet for La Favorita tortillas and a Mexican-style bakery. Their bakery goods are quite good, but very sweet. My favorites are pastry cupcake cases filled with custard. The pastries also come with apple or raspberry filling.

Their burritos are homemade and they have a selection of Mexican specialties like masa mixta, which is used to make tamales, corn husks to put the tamale mix into, ground chile, dried, diced shrimp (cameròn), and mixes for hominy and menudo.

There are Mexican spices, hot sauce, chicharrones, and of course fresh tortillas and tostadas.

The staff are always friendly and efficient, and they work very hard when it's busy, running back and forth to fill orders for the bakery and restaurant.

Mexidans

2101 Larimer 295-1773
Daily, 8 am–6 pm.

On the corner of 21st and Larimer, Mexidan's is in a neighborhood where there are more bars and pawn shops than any other kinds of business. Daniel is the owner, but since he's not there I talk to Miguel, who is at first sure I'm from the health department or somewhere he's else he's not interested in talking to. A customer who speaks English is more than willing to translate, though, and once Miguel realizes that I'm not from any of the establishment harassment centers, he tells me all about his baked and takeout goods and even presses me to sample a few.

Miguel bakes everything himself. His Mexican breads, or bolillos, are sweet and good, with a nice crust and just the right touch of sweetness. His carnitas are pork, cooked to a chewy crust on the outside but tender and flavorful within. He has takeout burritos, tamales, menudo (Mexican tripe soup), tamales, tostadas and enchiladas. His customers all unite to sing the praises of his food, especially his burritos. He himself tells me through our volunteer interpreter about his empanaditas (pastry turnovers) of apple or pineapple and his pastels de chocolat–chocolate flavored pastries. I thought his brownies were good, though a little heavy on the frosting.

In the corner there's the usual rack of Mexican spices. Mexidan is great for carnitas and bolillos and my guess is that the burritos and tamales are pretty good too.

MEXICAN WEDDING COOKIES

1 cup butter, softened
3/4 cup cornstarch
1/2 cup powdered sugar
1 cup flour
1 teaspoon vanilla

Cream butter and add cornstarch, powdered sugar and flour, in that order. Add vanilla and chill for 1 hour. Shape into 1" balls and flatten each ball slightly with thumb. Bake on an ungreased cookie sheet at 350° 10–12 minutes or until firm but not browned.

Panaderia Guadalajara

2223 W. 32nd Avenue 477-9916
Daily, 7 am–8 pm.

This small, Mexican-style bakery is owned by Frank Gonzalez, who has been serving this North Denver community for about two years. He sells a variety of Mexican breads and cookies. His flautas, filled with raspberry jam, are especially good and flaky, and his cuernos (horns) and calvos are favorites with his customers.

The bakery also offers the obligatory selection of Mexican spices, like red chiles, chamomile and others, and they also have tortillas, chicharrones (pork rinds) and mole sauce. A charming custom in all the Mexican bakeries is to put your choice of goods on a tray with a pair of tongs, so that you can see exactly what you're buying. Then, when your purchases are complete, they're all put into a bag.

Mexican baked goods are very different from French or other European cakes or cookies. They are sweet and flaky, and often drier than the butter-rich European baked goods.

Panaderia Guadalajara is one of several Mexican-style bakeries in this neighborhood. Try them out and experience their unique taste and texture.

Panaderia Rodriguez I

6201 W. Alameda, Lakewood 232-5646

Panaderia Rodriguez II
2402 W. 32nd Avenue 455-1405
Daily, 7:30 am–10 pm.

It's confusing. Panaderia II is the original bakery, and that's the one I visited first. They have cakes for sale that look like individual layer cakes, creamy icing layered with a kind of pound cake/sponge cake, called pastelitos. They also have the usual Mexican-style cakes and cookies, all very fresh and attractive-looking. They make sandwiches, called tortas, of Mexican bread with ham or chorizo and cheese, and gorditas, which are hand-made tortillas, stuffed with meat or chorizo, beans, and green chile.

I find all this out through a customer who's kind enough to interpret for me, because the young woman behind the counter speaks no English at all. She's determined to be helpful, though, and asks around until she finds someone who can help us out!

When I visit Panaderia I, I meet Luis Rodriguez Jr., son of the owner. He shows me the range of their baked goods: cream cheese danishes, pineapple and apple empanadas, polvorones, raspberry flautas and other goodies. The cream puffs are called patos (ducks) because of their shape. They also have deli food–burritos, chicharrones, tamales and tortas as well. Luis explains to me that all their bakery goods are made fresh daily and that they also sell tortillas and tostadas. These are very nice bakeries, one of my favorites in the Mexican-style bakery category.

750 Santa Fe Drive 571-4720
Daily, 7 am–10 pm.

The whole time I'm in this bakery, which also serves Mexican food, they are bringing out fresh baked goods to replenish those that have been sold. Flautas, flan in pastry shells, empanadas, large cookies with the chocolate chips on top, cream horns filled with cream or custard–I try the flautas and the cream horns and find them tasty. The flautas are pastries rolled around raspberry or lemon filling. The cream horns have a more bread-like dough, and the custard filling is creamy and good. I'm tempted by the desserts, like flan, jello and a tiramisu-like mixture of custard and cake, but manage to resist this time.

Meanwhile, there are also bolillos, those small loaves of slightly sweet Mexican bread, and in the refrigerator case Mexican specialties like crema mexicana, nopalitos (cactus), chorizo and ranchero cacique cheese. The Mexican spices are more interesting than most I've seen, probably because they're more medicinal than culinary. They include valerian, arnica, sassafras (flowers and powder), guava leaf, whole nutmeg , walnut leaf and mullein.Valerian is the strongest herbal sedative there is. Arnica is used for sprains and bruises. Walnut leaf is believed to be good for skin and hair and mullein is used for coughs.

This is a nice place, with a lot going on both inside and outside. The neighborhood is teeming with life and energy. The clerk who helps me tries to explain things to me, which is very kind of him because he's so busy. This is the place to sample a variety of Mexican-style desserts and pastries.

Pasteleria del Norte

2643 W. 32nd Avenue 433-5171
Daily, 6 am–10 pm.

This bakery is right across the street from Rosales Bakery, and has many of the same kinds of baked goods. They have sweet breads shaped into little round loaves and sweet pastries shaped like horseshoes that are very inexpensive and good. There are also different kinds of cookies, including cinnamon and honey cookies, and empanadas (turnovers) filled with apple, cheese or pumpkin.

There's a rack of Mexican spices like oregano, chile de arbol, cumin and dried chiles. Chile de arbol is a small, orange-red dried chile, that when puréed has a lovely burnt orange color and a very hot, sharp chile flavor.

Rosales Mexican Bakery

2636 W. 32nd Avenue 458-8420
Daily, 6 am–10 pm.

This place is a real find! The bakery case has an amazing array of wonderful Mexican cookies, all for 25–35 cents each. They have marranitos, so-called because they're shaped like little piggies, which are a made from a kind of ginger-bread, and escobas, meaning brooms, which are flaky sugar pastry. Their cacahuates or peanut cookies are also named after their shape, and they're cookies in peanut-shaped halves, held together with an ample paste of frosting.

There are also polvorones sevil-lanos, which are Mexican wed-ding cookies, and payasos or clowns which are cookies made of multicolored dough: yellow and pink and beige. The yoyos are large, round cookies with frosting in the middle, covered with coconut, and they do look like big yoyos. There's also a huge slab of cajeta de membril-lo (quince jam) which is a regional specialty of the region in Mexico from which the

Rosales family comes. Their specialties are bolillos, which are small Mexican breads, and conchas (shell cookies).

In the refrigerator case are chorizo, and crema mexicana, which is Mexican whipping cream. They also sell tortillas. This bakery has been owned and operated by the Rosales family for 18 years. It's one of my favorite bakeries in this area.

Sexy Bakeries

Le Bakery Sensual

300 E. 6th Avenue (6th & Grant) 839-8100
Monday–Friday, 9:30 am–6 pm; Saturday & Sunday, 10 am–4 pm.

A sensual experience is guaranteed when you order a cake from Le Bakery Sensual, the sexiest bakery in town. John Spotts, the owner, is a former art student who has turned his talents to producing and decorating erotic and humorous cakes in flavors like spice, carrot and German chocolate. His decorations can be explicit, funny or romantic, according to your taste. The idea book showing some of John's greatest hits will give you a starting point for bachelor or bachelorette parties, anniversaries, special birthday parties, over-the-hill parties or even children's celebrations.

This store is unlike anything I've ever seen anywhere else, and you will be amazed as you feast your eyes on candies made of intimate body parts and see messages such as "Breast wishes on your birthday" atop cakes with anatomically correct females disporting themselves with indiscreet abandon! John has been creating his erotic masterpieces for the last twelve years and is glad to put together any kind of cake or candy you can imagine. There is also a collection of bawdy cards and gifts. Edible erotic art could be an idea whose time has come. If you have a friend or spouse who would appreciate a cake or gift that's truly one-of-a-kind, this is the place–maybe almost the only place–to get it.

Delicatessens

When you want something quick and flavorful, nothing beats deli food. We owe the diversity of deli foods that we can find around town to the European immigrants who came to this country and brought with them their own kinds of food. From Germany, sausage of all kinds, liverwurst, pumpernickel and beer, from Italy, pasta, olives, cheeses both hard for grating and soft, like ricotta, as well as lupini beans and sweet peppers. The Jewish immigrants brought lox and gefilte fish, the Scandinavians introduced us to smoked fish and herring and the Eastern Europeans engendered a variety of pickles, stuffed cabbage, marinated vegetables and their own varieties of sausage. And, of course, to greet them here in Colorado were the Hispanic immigrants, whose food was already blended with the ways and ingredients of the native Americans, making tamales, chorizo and salsas.

The delis I've visited around town are generally dedicated to providing top quality merchandise to their customers. They want to share their delight in good food, made the old-fashioned way, usually without preservatives, using the best quality ingredients and resulting in superior taste.

One thing I've learned in my quest for diverse and interesting food: never make anything if you can buy it and it's just as good. Delis offer the best proof of the wisdom of this belief.

American Delicatessens

East Coast Italian Deli

8998 E. Hampden Avenue (Hampden & Yosemite) 741-0908
Monday–Friday, 7 am–8 pm; Saturday, 8 am–5 pm.

Tucked away in a shopping center at Yosemite and Hampden is the fresh and tasty East Coast Deli. You may wonder why they're listed here instead of under Italian delis. The reason is that they seem more New York Italian than Italian Italian. Does that make sense?

Their authentic New York Italian subs come with many toppings, like fried onions and sweet peppers, just like back East. The bowls in the deli case are filled with fresh salads daily, and they vary with the season. I think the variety of salads is great, with offerings like shell pasta with broccoli, dill with cucumber and tomatoes, tabouli salad, Manhattan pasta with pepperoni and salami and something I've never seen before–spaghetti salad–spaghetti noodles with Italian dressing and red onions, cucumbers and tomatoes. Cole slaw, potato salad, twice-baked potatoes and deviled eggs–all made with loving care by two ladies with a combined 35 years of cooking experience. And in the winter, they offer great homemade soups, which change daily.

Italian dishes available to take out include spaghetti, lasagne, eggplant parmesan and ziti with meatballs or sausage. Desserts are all homemade and include fresh brownies, cookies, cheesecake, peach and apple cobbler and chocolate and banana mousse.

"People come from all over the city for our takeout," says owner George. "Sometimes they bring in their own containers so they can take our cooking to a potluck supper as their own!" With this kind of home cooking available, who can blame them?

Gold Star Sausage Company

2800 Walnut 295-6400
Monday–Friday, 6:30 am–2:30 pm. Closed Saturday & Sunday.

Gold Star only sells in bulk–which in their case means 10 lbs. plus of each item (some items are only sold in 23 or 25 lb. lots). However, they are willing to sell to the public if you're willing to buy in these kinds of quantities. Their main business is wholesale, selling hot dogs to street vendors and sausage and other meats to local supermarkets.

They have an amazing range of products: from Polish, German and Italian sausages, wieners, bratwurst and chorizo to braun- schweiger,

cooked spareribs, hot chicken wings and tamales. The company has been in Denver over 20 years and is owned by two part- ners, Bill Bolton and Ron Rue. If you have a large freezer and like to buy in quantity, you can save some money by shopping at Gold Star.

Mortensen's Gourmet-To-Go

5270 E. Arapahoe Road 773-6326 Fax: 773-6064
Monday–Friday, 7 am–5 pm; Saturday, 10 am–3 pm.
Closed Sunday.

I almost missed this little place, located in a shopping center on Holly and Arapahoe. But when I finally found it, I was amazed that they have such a variety of offerings. The chef and owner, Paul Mortensen, has a history of professional cooking that many chefs would envy. He graduated from the Culinary Institute of America, then worked in France and New York before moving to Colorado. He has breakfasts, salads, sandwiches, and all kinds of other gourmet take-out and catered foods. Hors d'oeu-

vres like lamb with fennel in phyllo dough, hoisin and orange duck, stuffed mushroom caps, quesadillas and seafood enchiladas with chipotle sauce are just a few of the dishes he offers.

He has lasagne to go, as well as box lunches and other dishes you can pick up straight from his freezer. You can get almost anything delivered, too. French, Mexican and Italian food are Paul's specialties. Call first to make sure he has what you want, or have him send you his extensive list of possibilities!

Our Daily Bread

12201 E. Arapahoe Road, Englewood 790-1217
Monday–Friday, 6:30 am–3:30 pm; Saturday, 9:30 am–2 pm.
Closed Sunday.

This little bakery/deli out in the back of beyond is a place in transition. Recently bought by a Korean couple, it offers both burritos and egg drop soup! Later they plan to add Korean-style barbecue and teriyaki, as well as vegetable fried rice. But the previous owner taught them to make Mexican specialties, so they'll be keeping those, as well.

Meanwhile, there's still the standing lunch special, which includes a drink and side orders: a burrito with guacamole combination. They have a breakfast burrito that sounds tempting, served with sausage, ham or bacon. And their salads are eclectic–potato, pasta, taco salad or oriental, to name a few.

The people who work here are so full of good will and hard work, they can't help but succeed. Look for many more kinds of dishes to emerge here in the near future, as Sung Le and his wife Sonya find their way in the deli food business.

Rockies Deli & Bakery

1630 Welton 892-5802
Monday–Friday, 6:30 am–3 pm; Saturday, 8 am–2 pm.
Closed Sunday.

Rockies has fresh bagels, including honey oat flavor, which I haven't come across before, and enormous muffins. These muffins would make an entire breakfast! They also sell loaves of bread of various kinds, pizza by the slice, Boar's Head meats, like pastrami, turkey breast, ham and corned beef, and side dishes like potato salad and cole slaw. They serve breakfast and sandwiches, soups and salads for lunch and also offer catering.

Around the corner, on the Sixteenth Street Mall, is Rockies Cafe, which shares a bakery with Rockies Deli, and is owned by the same people, Jim and Nancy Turley. The cafe has espresso and cappuccino, and some scones and salads that I didn't see at the deli. They also sell coffee beans. Service was very nice and friendly at both places, and everything was fresh and attractive-looking.

S & K Deli

9138 W. 6th Avenue, Lakewood 233-6352
Monday–Friday, 7 am–8 pm; Saturday, 8 am–8 pm;.
Sunday, 9 am–3 pm. (Winter hours: 9 am–6 pm.)

Just like the British missionaries who brought their teapots, tea, jams and other accoutrements of "civilization" with them when they explored darkest Africa, Kathy and Syd Robinson decided that when they couldn't find anything resembling the Long Island delis they had grown up with, they'd better just start their own!

"The closest thing we found to a Long Island deli was Seven Eleven," says Syd.

"That just didn't cut it," his wife, Kathy, answers.

So here in the wilds of Lakewood, right off the Garrison exit from Sixth Avenue, S&K Deli was born. They have bratwurst, bologna and pastrami and they make their own potato salad, macaroni salad and cole slaw. The many homemade items include egg salad, ham salad and meatballs. Syd and Kathy experiment, listen to their customers and try to figure out how to please them. Their potato salad is really delicious.

Syd and Kathy also serve cheesecake, muffins and pastries. If you're homesick for a Long Island deli, this is a place to try.

WHITE BEAN DIP

2 lbs. white beans
1 bay leaf
1 Kaffir lime leaf
6 cloves garlic, mashed (divided)
4 sprigs fresh thyme
1 cup white wine
5 cups strong chicken stock
1 cup olive oil
Salt and pepper to taste
Few drops hot chili oil

Soak beans in large pan of water overnight. Drain. Put beans, bay leaf, Kaffir lime leaf, 3 garlic cloves, thyme, wine and chicken stock in large kettle and bring to a boil. Cook almost 2 hours, until beans are tender, adding a little water if too much evaporates. Heat olive oil and gently sauté garlic. Add chili oil. Drain beans and purée in blender, adding olive oil mixture slowly. Serve with triangles of pita or naan.

Star Market Deli & Catering

2357 E. Evans (Evans & University) 777-0495
Monday–Friday, 8 am–6 pm; Saturday, 9 am–4 pm. Closed Sunday.

If you're looking for out-of-this-world carrot cake, this is the place to visit! They make their own carrot cake, zucchini bread, banana nut bread and banana bundt cake, as well as their own poppyseed cake. But the carrot cake is truly spectacular. Owner Michael Schettler

also offers box lunches, catering, and does weddings and party trays as well as wedding and birthday cakes. His wife decorates the cakes. Recently, they've started creating wedding cakes decorated with beads and pearls.

They have subs, salads and the usual deli meats and cheeses. They carry Boar's Head brand (it's very good quality)–"I'm from New York," explains Michael. Where they know about deli, is the unspoken end to that sentence. There's a stoplight in the middle of the eating area. "They closed down the street outside for nearly a year, widening it," Michael says. "So when they were almost done, we threw a construction party. They gave me the stoplight and the street sign from Evans and University."

Star Market used to be an old supermarket, back in the days when there were neighborhood markets. There are even photos of customers from those days, put up on the ends of the aisles. They've also added to them under the new regime, with pictures of the present owners and customers. This deli's a pleasure to walk into. Everything's fresh and attractive and the service is friendly. And that carrot cake....

Tignon's Deli

1604 E. 17th Avenue (17th & Franklin) 322-7874
Monday–Saturday, 10 am–7 pm. Closed Sunday.

Chicken atjlimojili catches my eye as I'm looking at the specialties on the board. That's quite a mouthful–in several senses of the word, since this chicken sandwich is very hot. The special sauce is from the Guinea coast, according to owner Janis Lewis. She also makes a turkey d. avocat sandwich, which is very spicy because of the spicy avocado sauce. "I love Caribbean food," says Janis. "And Caribbean food and African food are very similar, because the slaves brought their cooking style with them." Her West African lemonade is called lemouroudji.

She makes hot wings with dirty rice, a New Orleans recipe, and New Orleans bread pudding with pineapple raisin sauce as the dessert of the day occasionally. This is a very attractive little deli close to the hospital district on Seventeenth Avenue. All the dishes in the deli case are made right here: seafood salads, potato salad, cucumber salad and garden vegetable salad. There's a very light torte for dessert, as well as a pastacio salad, which Janis describes as a dessert salad.

Janis runs the deli with her partner Estel Lowe, a quiet gentleman with a lovely smile. She obviously enjoys her work. Tignon's Deli is attractive and inviting. This is the place to try unusual and spicy dishes from Africa and the Caribbean.

CARIBBEAN RED BEANS & RICE

1 lb. hot Italian sausage meat
1 large onion, chopped fine
1 large green pepper, diced
1 large red pepper, diced
1 large yellow pepper, diced
4 cloves garlic, crushed
2 bay leaves
3 Kaffir lime leaves (available in Thai groceries)
2 teaspoons oregano
2 tablespoons hot pepper sauce
2–15 oz. cans red kidney beans, drained
2–3 large, ripe bananas, sliced

4 cups cooked brown rice

recipe continued across ➡

German Delicatessens

Alpine Sausage Company

1272 W. Alaska Place 778-0886
Monday–Friday, 9:30 am–6:30 pm; Saturday, 9:30 am–4 pm.
Closed Sunday.

Alpine Sausage Company is the place to visit if you want to know about sausage. Bertram Frei, originally from Switzerland, has been making his own sausage here for 21 years. And what sausage he makes–each kind with its own distinct flavor and texture, each kind subtly different and delicious. Swiss wieners, alpine bratwurst, knock-wurst, ticinellas Italian, Louisiania hot links, madridos chorizo, Slovenian blood and rice sausage, Nürnberger bratwurst, apple saucisson (saucisson is French for sausage), Schueblig, Polish kielbasa... the list continues. He even makes British bangers! However, Bert adds his own touch to the bangers: onions. In my opinion, it makes them much tastier than the real British bangers!

Bert gets into a long conversation with a regular customer about the virtues and vices of nitrites. He can make sausage without nitrites, of course, he says, and many of his sausages don't have nitrites. But for the smoked sausages to be preserved properly, the nitrites are necessary.

Bert's sausages are delicious. He has many loyal customers, and for good reason. These are real, old-world sausages, as various and interesting as their origins.

Brown sausage meat in skillet over medium heat, breaking up with wooden spoon. Add onion as sausage browns. Then add peppers, garlic, oregano, Kaffir lime leaves and bay leaves. Cook about 10 minutes. When vegetables are softened but not mushy, add beans and hot sauce. Cook over low heat 15 minutes. Add sliced bananas and cook 10–15 minutes longer. Serve over the rice. Serves 4.

Bender's Brat Haus

1534 E. 6th Avenue 344-2648
Monday–Friday, 10 am–5 pm; Saturday, 10 am–4 pm.
Closed Sunday.

Beverly and Chuck Bender have been making their own bratwurst from an old family recipe of Chuck's for the past 17 years. Chuck's grandparents came from Germany and settled in Sheboygan, Wisconsin. When he opened the Brat Haus in 1976, Chuck started using the old family recipe. Beverly kept her outside job till the place was beginning to make money, and then she quit and started working with her husband.

They make their own sauerkraut, German potato salad and also a krautburger sandwich consisting of ground beef, cabbage and onion. They sell the brats both cooked and ready to eat and cook-it-yourself. Beverly advises me that it would cost quite a bit less to cook it myself! I figure my culinary talents are just about up to it, so that's what I do. Both the brats and the sauerkraut are nothing short of spectacular. A little German mustard and I would be waltzing to the Blue Danube and imagining myself back on the Hohehzollern Bridge over the Rhine in Cologne, where I met my first husband when I was just a high school graduate from England and he was an American undergraduate. We lived on bratwurst then–in fact, we probably sampled every bratwurst available in Cologne, so I consider myself something of an expert.

If you want to wash your brat down with a beer, that's possible at Bender's, since you can eat at the restaurant as well as take out. This place is totally unique. The people are wonderful and the food is good, straightforward and inexpensive.

Continental Delicatessen

250 Steele 388-3354
Monday–Friday, 9–5; Saturday, 9–4. Closed Sunday.

When you walk into this upscale deli in the Cherry Creek area, you're greeted by German oompah music. The deli makes its own sausage at another location, so the variety is enormous: knackwurst, bratwurst, veal brats, frankfurters, wieners–all freshly made. They also have a variety of German hams, like bauernschinken and bierschinken, summer sausage, liverwurst, braunschweiger and salami. The potato salad and sauerkraut are also homemade, and there is a great selection of imported cheeses, including Tilsit, Jarlsberg, Swiss Vacherin, Edam and Gruyère.

Unusual ingredients include raw poppy seed and German table butter, as well as many varieties of dark German deli breads like German rye, linseed rye and Schwartzbrot (literally, black bread). I've never seen such a complete selection of Knorr soups, bouillons and mixes, including dessert mixes. There are many kinds of preserves and jams, and more unusual spreads like chocolate hazelnut spread, rose hip preserves from Switzerland and linden and verbena herb teas.

If you're looking for German foods, this is a good place to find them. Their selection is broad, and it's a pleasing store to browse in.

European Delights

8440 W. Colfax, Lakewood 237-5655
Monday–Saturday, 10 am–6 pm. Closed Sunday.

This old world-style delicatessen is a family business, run by Elvira and Victor Marusin. Elvira is Polish and Victor is Czech. Together they keep alive the tradition of excellence in food preparation and service and work hard to keep up the old ways of doing things. They make many different kinds of Polish sausage, from old family recipes. European Delights has been open for ten years. Elvira and Victor came to the United States with nothing but a couple of suitcases, no money and no English. They believe in making sausage the traditional way, with no substitutes.

I tasted the sausage, and it's unique and quite wonderful.

They also sell other meats like pastrami and roast beef, and cheeses like provolone and Swiss. They have homemade German rye bread and a selection of gourmet jams, peppers and pickles.

Customers who have tasted the food here keep coming back for more. Once people taste the difference between Victor and Elvira's traditional recipes and "the other stuff", the other stuff just won't do any more, according to Elvira. She'll put together party trays for all occasions and give you great service besides.

728 Peoria, Aurora (Hoffmann Heights Shopping Center) 344-5488
Monday, 8 am–6 pm; Tuesday–Friday, 8 am–9 pm;
Saturday, 9 am–9 pm; Sunday, 11 am–4 pm.

Helga's has a great selection of German sausage, like bratwurst, knockwurst, leberwurst (liverwurst), bierwurst (beer sausage), and also some excellent ham, like bauernschinken and smoked ham. The deli offers several kinds of salami and summer sausage and a small but excellent selection of cheese: mild and Tilsit Havarti, Edam, beer cheese and Emmenthaler, which is a superior kind of Swiss cheese, the original Swiss cheese that's actually made in Switzerland. Helga's is a family-owned operation, and Helga's mother makes most of the cakes, which are totally authentic: apfelkuchen, bienenstich, streuselkuchen and apple and cherry strudel, as well as Black Forest cake and cream tortes.

Everyone is very helpful and will tell you all about the items in the deli case and pronounce them with very authentic German accents! There is also a selection of German canned and packaged products, such as canned sauerkraut, hot mustards, jams, gravy and hunter sauce mixes, dried soups from Maggi and Knorr and some German and Swiss chocolates.

Cake mixes include Black Forest cake and Frankfurt cream cake, and there are several packaged herbal teas, like linden blossom and rose hip. Anyone who hasn't tried linden blossom tea is missing a real treat. When I worked in a chateau in France for a summer, at the tender age of 17, I first sampled this excellent

tisane by pretending to be sick when I was actually simply too tired to keep working 12 hour days without a break! Its restorative powers almost made my drudgery worthwhile. (Perhaps the added rum also helped?)

Helga's also has a variety of fruit syrups, mineral waters and a small selection of German toiletries, like Kölnischwasser (eau de cologne) and original European Nivea. Germany weekly news magazines are available for those who speak German.

Karl's F.F. Delicatessen

6878 S. Yosemite, Englewood 694-0260
Monday–Friday, 9 am–5:30 pm; Saturday, 9 am–3 pm.
Closed Sunday.

This bright and cheerful German deli has an upbeat atmosphere. I'm greeted with a smile by Dieter, who works here and is a friend of the owners, Karl and Ursula Boschen. Obviously, he's here because he likes it, and it shows! A variety of German sausage and ham is on display in the deli case: blutwurst, schinkenwurst, bratwurst, knackwurst, Westphalian ham, and bierschinken. There's also homemade potato salad, sauerkraut and sometimes, in summer, red cabbage. In the winter homemade soups are available. Each day there's a hot plate special: a German wurst with potato salad and sauerkraut or red cabbage.

Imported smoked ham, smoked eel and mackerel are some of the German specialties you can find here, along with imported beers. Dieter tells me that they have just found an American sweet butter that's equal to the German butter–a great improvement since it's available far less expensively. There's a sign in German informing everyone about this, since it's people who lived in Germany and were able to get this wonderful butter who want to buy it now that its equivalent is available here. German cheeses are also available, including soft Bavarian cheese.

There are some shelves with German products that prove interesting. Imported sweets, chocolates, many kinds of German mustards, pickles, zweiback, lots of luscious-looking German jams like lingonberry, syrups such as raspberry, blackberry and sour cherry, and herb teas: chamomile and lemongrass. There are also some German creams and lotions, including the European version of Nivea, which some of my European friends still prefer over the American version.

Karl's has a patio if you want to sit out and enjoy the sun while eating, if the weather cooperates. With its blue-and-white umbrellas, it manages to evoke a European sidewalk cafe. This is a pleasant and attractive place to visit. (It took me a while to figure out that the "F.F." means fast food!)

Presidential Food Facts

President James Buchanan served sauerkraut and mashed potatoes at parties at his home in Wheatland, Pennsylvania.

Italian Delicatessens

Belfiore's Italian Sausage

3161 W. 38th Avenue, Denver 455-4653
Monday–Saturday, 8:30 am–5:30 pm. Closed Sunday.

At this small, family Italian market, they make their own Italian sausage, both mild and hot. They have homemade fresh pasta: gnocchi, ravioli and tortellini. Their Italian cheeses include Romano Pecorino, Asiago, casa cavallo (a cheese very similar to provolone) and imported provolone. They also have salami, pepperoni, olive oils, Italian lupini beans and sweet roasted peppers. Theresa, the owner, is very helpful, and knowledgeable about the different kinds of meats, pastas and cheeses. It's such a delight to talk to someone who knows about the ingredients and products she sells, and can give good advice about how to use them!

Here you'll find a selection of pastas, balsamic vinegar, bread sticks and biscotti, and Perugina chocolates. Since it's right next door to El Alamo, the Italian/Mexican bakery, you could pop into both and in a jiffy you'd have the ingredients for a great Italian meal!

Carbone Italian Sausage

1221 W. 38th Avenue 455-2893
Monday–Saturday, 8 am–5 pm. Closed Sunday.

The wonderful aromatic odor in the air is fennel from the fresh sausage they're making, and it's truly delicious. Here they make all their own sausage–hot and mild Italian, and owner Nick Leonardo shows me great coils of them, fresh today. Nick has been operating the deli at this location for 20 years, and the store itself has probably been here for over 50 years. This is the old Italian section of North Denver, after all.

As well as sausage, there's pepperoni, sopressata, and other meats, as well as cheeses like ricotta, fontinella, scamorza and goat cheese. There are many kinds of peppers, brightly colored and fresh-looking in jars along the top of the counter. There are John's brand gourmet pastas in the freezer case: manicotti and ravioli, among others. A gnocchi maker, an espresso maker and a pizzelle baker are also available. There are olive oils and vinegars, a selection of different olives and a selection of Italian cookies: palm leaves, biscotti and also bread sticks.

Deli Italia

1990 Wadsworth 238-7815 Fax: 238-7815
Monday–Saturday, 9 am–6 pm. Closed Sunday.

One of the most surprising things about this attractive Italian deli is that Ricardo makes his own fresh mozzarella cheese. It's quite different from the bland stuff you find in the supermarket–creamy, tasty, with just a hint of smoke flavoring. Sometimes he puts some prosciutto or a cherry tomato inside the fresh cheese balls, so that they will slice beautifully for party trays! It's quite an art, but he makes it look easy.

Ricardo is also very interested in different shapes of pasta. He boasts over 100 different ones, and is very knowledgeable about them. For example, I knew that orecchiette meant "little ears" but I didn't know that they are also called priests' ears, after the ears that hear so many secrets in confession! Ricardo knows many such fascinating stories. He also has the largest pasta I've ever seen, called candele. I couldn't imagine how you'd cook them, until he suggested they'd be good cooked up in the hot tub!!

Deli Italia also has many frozen filled pastas, many of which haven't even been labeled for retail sale. And there are pesto and other kinds of sauce to put over your gnocchi and ravioli. There's a whole aisle devoted to cookies, crackers and candies from Italy, and a very good selection of olive oils and balsamic vinegars.

The deli case is filled with Italian hams and sausages: pepperoni, capocollo, porcetta, mortadella–and there are many kinds of olives and several different kinds of homemade olive salad. The cheese selection is good, and includes Asiago, Romano, Parmesan and many

more. One of my favorite beverage choices is a small bottle of Italian non-alcoholic aperitif, and Ricardo has a half dozen different kinds. They're very refreshing, although some of them may be too bitter for most American tastes.

Deli Italia carries small espresso makers and press coffee makers, as well as some Italian dishes and glasses. Their bread is good and they even have espressos, lattes and other specialty coffee drinks.

Lonardo's Italian Sausage Meat Deli

7585 W. Florida, Lakewood 985-3555
Monday–Saturday, 8 am–6 pm. Closed Sunday.

Big wedges of Asiago, Parmesan and Romano jostle ricotta and marscapone and even tiramisu in the refrigerator section of this Italian deli. There are also many fresh pastas, like agnoletti, tagliatelle and gnocchi, and fresh-made chorizo as well as hot and mild Italian sausage.

Carmine Lonardo and his family run this deli on the corner of Florida and Wadsworth in Lakewood. He sells quality fresh meats, like steaks and chops, in small quantities or as one of several bulk packages of meat or meat, poultry and sausage. These package deals are posted above the counter, with prices. You can also buy

capocollo and sopressata and other Italian meats, and several kinds of fresh Italian bread.

There are many rows of peppers, hot, mild, cherry, roasted and in various other incarnations. Also there are marinated mushrooms, Italian giardiniera, and a good selection of olive oils and balsamic vinegars. There's an entire section of different kinds of spaghetti sauce, lupini beans and other Italian specialties.

If you're looking for packages of Italian cookies or Italian chocolates, you'll find those too. The whole family helps out here, and everyone's cheerful and hardworking.

Mariano's Italian Deli

6813 Lowell   428-8946
Monday–Saturday, 9 am–6:30 pm. Closed Sunday.

This tiny place in a strip shopping center on the corner of 68th & Lowell advertises that it's the "home of the bucket of pasta" on a sign in the window. Apparently the bucket is available to serve three or six, and is a specialty of the house. David Mariano has been supervising the running of this family business for the past six years, and there has been an Italian deli with at least two previous owners at this same location, according to David's son. They make their own sausage here, and also bake their own Italian bread (regular loaves and braids), turnovers, pies, cakes, strudels and more.

They have a selection of Italian sausages and salamis, olives, cheeses, including goat cheese, and some pastas, olive oil and other Italian specialties. Their cannolis are also homemade and delicious! This is a nice little deli with friendly people and good home-made food. They've catered to the north Denver Italian community for many years–now it's time for the rest of the world to discover them.

Old Fashioned Italian Deli

395 W. Littleton Boulevard, Littleton   794-1402
Monday–Friday, 8:30 am–7:30 pm; Saturday, 9 am–6:30 pm.
Closed Sunday.

Black and white photos of Marilyn Monroe and several rows of caps with different sports insignias grace the walls of this Littleton eatery, where you can get six foot subs or a whole cheesecake with only two days' notice! Their sandwiches have names like the Terminator and the Destroyer, which makes me wonder what they might do to your insides–but only for a minute. This place has salamis, pepperoni, Romano, Gorgonzola, and all the Italian deli accompaniments, as well as many kinds of imported pasta, balsamic vinegar, olive oils, frozen tortellini... as George Miller said, "The trouble with eating Italian food is that five or six days later you're hungry again."

The deli is owned by Tom Panzarella and his partner Dave. They opened the Old Fashioned Italian Deli in March, 1986 and haven't looked back. Tom used to be an air traffic controller, but always wanted to own an Italian deli (must have been his Sicilian ancestry coming out!) so he worked at a Polish-American deli for a while after the air traffic controllers' strike made it impossible for him to work in that field anymore. He decided to open his own place, found a partner, and the rest is history.

Roberto's Sausage

1415 E. 58th 297-0370
Monday–Friday, 6 am–4 pm; Saturday, 10 am–2 pm.
Closed Sunday.

Roberto's seems to be in an unusual location for such a friendly little deli–until you realize that they cater to the industrial areas all around them. However, this is not at all a greasy spoon–it's a nicely decorated, clean and attractive place that makes its own sausage–German and Italian, fresh twice a week, and ships it all over the country, as well as offering fresh pasta salads, corned beef, turkey breast, lasagne, spaghetti and several hearty soups in season.

Party trays, appetizer and relish trays and even 6 foot sandwiches are available here. The place is run by owner Marvin Feist (yes, I know it's called Roberto's, but Marvin actually claims German ancestry), ably assisted by his manager Concetta Rotello, who is Italian!

Portions are generous, and they use only quality meats. It's really a find, and shines against its industrial background.

PESTO

1 cup Parmesan cheese
1 whole bulb garlic
1 large, fresh bunch basil
1 pound pine nuts
3 cups olive oil
1/4 cup salt & pepper or to taste

Peel garlic bulb and cloves. Slice garlic cloves. Sauté in olive oil until golden brown and drain. Wash fresh basil. Soak in ice water 3 times to remove grit. Toast pine nuts in oven until light brown. In food processor, add alternately olive oil, basil, garlic, pine nuts, salt and pepper. Finished pesto should be the consistency of wet oatmeal. Don't over-purée. Taste should be strong–it will mellow when tossed with pasta.

Tony's Italian Sausage and Deli

3855 Wadsworth, Wheat Ridge 420-1557
Monday–Friday, 8 am–7 pm; Saturday, 8 am–6 pm. Closed Sunday.

This Italian deli has only been in business a year, but it seems to be flourishing. Tony and his family make their own hot and mild Italian sausage, and there is a wide choice of Italian and American meats, like turkey breast, roast beef, Genoa salami, hard salami, prosciutto, hot ham and capocollo, as well as cheeses like Asiago, provolone, Parmesan, Romano and fontinella.

Tony's has an unusually comprehensive selection of frozen homemade ready-to-serve items. These include frozen meat balls, focaccia, pizza, spaghetti sauce, lentil soup, cabbage rolls, stuffed eggplant, stuffed calamari and family packs of lasagne to serve 4 or 10. John's gourmet brand of filled pastas–ravioli, tortellini and such–are available and there are jars of hot peppers, lupini beans, olive oils and other Italian grocery products. They make their own pizzelles, which is somewhat unusual.

Their Italian sausage is excellent, and I'm looking forward to trying some of their takeout food, since they assure me they're all made from grandma's Italian recipes.

Valente's Deli Bakery

7250 Meade, Westminster 429-0590
Monday–Saturday, 8 am–5 pm. Closed Sunday.

A huge sign on the north side of 72nd Avenue makes sure you don't miss Valente's, just two blocks west of Lowell. Somehow the place itself is smaller than I expected, given the size of the sign! They have lots of different breads, including some unusual ones like pepperoni cheddar and three cheese bread, as well as the usual kinds of light rye and sourdough. There are also sweet things like turnovers and cookies.

The deli has meats, deli-sliced bacon, pastrami, corned beef, capocollo and the like, and Italian cheeses like Romano and Asiago. They make their own Italian sausage and there are several kinds of homemade deli salads: macaroni, egg, four bean and an especially delicious-looking olive garden salad.

The frozen food section has white-paper wrapped meats labeled chicken and steak, just like in someone's home freezer.

They also have frozen tamales and noodles. There is the usual selection of pastas and pasta sauces, although some of the sauces look more interesting than usual. One brand is called Classico and the sweet peppers and onion sounds particularly good!

Vito's Italian Deli

9304-B W. 58th Avenue, Arvada 940-8042
Tuesday–Thursday & Saturday, 9 am–6 pm; Friday, 9 am–7 pm;
Sunday, 10 am–3 pm. Closed Monday.

Two guys from New York started this deli–George Militello and Paul LoNigro. George lived near Paul's dad in New York and they were friends. George always wanted a business like this, where he could carry top-of-the-line Italian specialties and imported pastas. So when he retired from being a sea captain, George teamed up with Paul and they opened Vito's.

They make their own sausage here–hot, mild, sweet, and sweet and hot. They also make fresh cheese with parsley, which is very popular in New York, on request, in quantities of 5 lbs. or more. Also available are their own pastas and sauces, including pestos, and they carry several different kinds of imported pastas.

There's a good selection of Italian meats and cheeses, including several different kinds of capocollo: hot, sweet, and hot peppered; hot calabrese salami, three kinds of prosciutto and imported Romano and scamorze cheeses.

George showed me the special cooler they have for dry sausage, to keep it at exactly the right temperature year-round.

George and Paul also have a selection of Italian machines, including pasta makers, graters and cappuccino makers. They've only been open about a year, but they're learning as they go, doing what they love. Let's hope these two guys from New York find their niche here in Denver.

Jewish & Kosher Delicatessens

The Bagel Delicatessen

6217 E. 14th (14th & Krameria) 322-0350
Monday–Friday, 7:30 am–8 pm; Saturday, 8 am–8 pm;
Sunday, 8 am–5 pm.

6439 East Hampden (Hampden & Monaco) 756-6667
Monday–Friday, 7 am–7:30 pm; Saturday & Sunday, 8 am–7:30 pm.

These are old-fashioned kosher delis, with all the things Jewish kids remember from their childhoods: lox, smoked whitefish, whipped cream cheese, meat and potato knishes, and cheese blintzes. Joe and Rhoda Kaplan run the Bagel Delis, which have takeout and are also restaurants. They bologna, mozzarella and Muenster, roast beef, corned beef, halvah and homemade stuffed peppers or lasagne. Gefilte fish is also available, along with that great horseradish colored with beet juice that always goes with it. And, best of all, how about a kosher dill pickle to chew on? They have

do, of course, have bagels, and they also have strudel, lemon bars, carrot cake and even flan!

You can buy borscht and them in jars, but I like the ones straight out of the barrel (they don't actually have a barrel any more, but it's close).

East Side Kosher Deli

5475 Leetsdale 322-9862
Monday–Thursday, 8:30 am–9 pm; Friday, 8:30 am–2 pm;
Sunday, 9 am–7:30 pm. Closed Saturday.

Mel and Irma Weiss run this kosher (not just kosher-style) deli and they have all the "Jewish delights" my first mother-in-law introduced me to when I first came to Chicago and the United States: noodle kugel, herring, pastrami, corned beef, chopped liver, chicken soup with matzoh balls–as well as fresh, home-made pastries like strudel and apple dumplings. The three bean salad, chopped liver, tuna salad and soup with matzoh balls are all homemade.

For those who hanker for gefilte fish with that wonderful horseradish sauce colored with beet juice, it's here. Among the kosher meats like rib eye roasts and whole briskets I found kishke–that wonderful addition to a Jewish holiday meal that has no equal. I was interested to find grapeseed oil, as well as more expected things like kosher salad dressings, cookies like animal crackers and mandeltoast, prune butter and other kosher items.

Their apple dumplings are terrific, and all their baked goods look fresh and wonderful. This is a nice place to shop for baked goods and Jewish specialty items. And, in case you or someone you love has a lactose intolerance, in general, kosher bakeries are great places to buy baked goods without milk in them. Since kosher dietary laws don't allow eating meat and milk at the same meal, most Jewish baked goods are made so that they can be served with either–and therefore have no milk! (The label pareve means without milk, so you can find other goods without milk this way in other stores too.)

New York Deli News

7105 E. Hampden 759-4741 Fax: 759-5055
Monday–Thursday, 7 am–10 pm; Friday & Saturday, 7 am–11 pm.
Sunday 7 am–10 pm.

This kosher-style deli has a sign in front that says, "Leaving Denver. Entering New York." Everything here is either home-made or from New York–the bagels ("The water in Brooklyn is different. So they boil the bagels there and then send them to us to bake."), the corned beef, the chocolate killer cake. There's a great selection of "Jewish delights." And delightful they are–Nova lox, whitefish, sable fish, gefilte fish, borscht, matzo ball soup, challah (egg bread). They have knishes and blintzes too.

Their desserts look equally delectable, and include the aforementioned chocolate killer cake, New York cheesecake, apple strudel, and black and whites–halfmoon sponge cakes, iced half in chocolate, half in vanilla. But best of all, to me, are those large kosher pickles. Walking out, the sign reads,

"Leaving New York. Entering Denver."

Plaza Deli

2456 S. Colorado   756-5489
Monday–Friday, 7 am–8 pm; Saturday, 7am–6 pm;
Sunday, 10 am–3 pm.

Entering the Plaza Deli is like going back in time. But that's hardly surprising, considering it's been in business for 38 years. The walls are covered with a gallery of old Jewish families from the 1870's on, many of them from the Jewish Historical Society. Here is Rabbi Elias Hillkowitz, who came to Denver in 1890, and the wedding of Mr. and Mrs. Sam Grimes in 1892. Here, too, is Philip Hornbein, in a photo taken around 1917. He was the lawyer who led the fight against the Ku Klux Klan in Colorado.

The Plaza Deli is kosher-style and has some kosher items, but it's been owned for the last 13 years by Lou and Hermine Schechs. Lou is originally from Bavaria, and enjoys operating a deli that has become a fixture in the neighborhood. "People who lived around here as children come back to see if the food's still as good," he says with a smile. "I don't think they're disappointed." Their most popular items are corned beef, pastrami and lox. Their soups and salads are all homemade.

70-80% of the people who eat here are repeat customers, so be prepared to get hooked if you try it. It's a nice deli with a warm atmosphere and an enormous menu. Enjoy!

3921 W. Colfax 623-7690
Monday–Friday, 11 am–4 pm. Closed Saturday & Sunday.

Mrs. Rosen has run this deli for a good number of the forty eight years it's been in the neighborhood. It's kosher-style, and used to be kosher until five or six years ago. She has corned beef, pastrami, roast beef, salami, turkey, lox and cream cheese, not to mention potato salad and the chili they make themselves. They claim to have the best Reuben sandwich in the city of Denver, and I wouldn't doubt it. They also carry kosher liver sausage. Mrs. Rosen is a friendly hostess, always willing to chat if she has time. Try the Reuben or the chili.

Mexican Delicatessens

CHICKEN WITH POSOLE

1/4 cup olive oil
2 large onions, chopped
4 cloves garlic, mashed or chopped
6 large carrots, sliced
3 large potatoes, chopped into 1" cubes
3 stalks celery, chopped
3-1/2–4 lb. chicken, washed
6 cups chicken stock
4 sprigs fresh oregano or 1 teaspoon dried oregano
1 cup dry white wine
1–29 oz. can white hominy, drained
Salt and ground black pepper, to taste
Up to 2 tablespoons crushed red chile

Heat olive oil in large heavy casserole. Sweat garlic and onion in oil over medium low heat 10 minutes. Add celery and carrots, cooking 5–7 minutes. Add potatoes and cook 5 minutes longer. Add wine, stirring to deglaze the pan. Pour in chicken broth and other ingredients except hominy. Put chicken into casserole and bring to boil. Simmer 25–45 minutes until chicken juices run clear when pierced. Lift chicken out of casserole and cool on a plate. Debone chicken and discard skin and bones. Return meat, cut into bite-sized pieces, to casserole. Add hominy and heat gently. Serves 4–6.

Lala's Gourmet Mexican Deli

3609 W. 32nd 455-1117
Monday–Friday, 11 am–7 pm; Saturday, 10 am–4 pm.
Closed Sunday.

Ezekiel and Lala Lucero own this Mexican delicatessen with their son Santiago. It's located near the corner of 32nd and Lowell, in a charming little district of shops, coffeehouses and restaurants. Lala's is famous for tamales, and now offers vegetarian as well as the regular pork, smothered with red or green chile. They make their own chorizo, from a recipe that's been in the family for 100 years. Zeke is experimenting with different flavors of chorizo, and expects to perfect a rum flavor, beer flavor and cilantro flavor very soon.

They also make their own tinga, a kind of barbecued shredded turkey, marinated in a special sauce with longaniza sausage. Their carne adovada is excellent. Zeke also makes his own queso fresco (fresh cheese) a soft table cheese that can also be used in quesadillas and other Mexican dishes. Salsas, red and green chile and tamales are available for takeout in half pints, pints and quarts, as are rice, beans and guacamole. Chorizo, longaniza, carne adovada and tinga are available by the pound.

Lala's is the only store I know of in town where

they make their own chipotle peppers (from jalapenos, ripened, dried and smoked). The taste is fiery but sweet, quite different from those you buy in a can. Lala's flan is one of the best I've tasted–cool and creamy, with a wonderful caramel sauce.

Call beforehand if you have your heart set on something special, to be sure they have it in stock–for example, restaurants sometimes buy up their entire inventory of flan–and you don't want to be disappointed!

Pasta

Pasta Pasta Pasta

278 Fillmore, Cherry Creek 377-2782
Monday–Friday, 10 am–5:30 pm; Saturday, 10 am–4 pm.
Closed Sunday.

Patti and Lisa Miller have been running this pasta takeout and deli for over nine years. They make all their own pastas, and have egg and spinach, tortellini and ravioli available all the time. They will also make other flavors–almost any flavor your want, really, if you're buying ten pounds or more. Patti and Lisa sell a good deal of their pasta wholesale, in large quantities, anyway.

They have many pastas available by the pound and pastas and other dishes prepared and available for takeout. The selection varies daily, or you can call and request a special dish and they'll be glad to prepare it for you. For example, one day some of the available dishes are eggplant parmesan, rigatoni with tomato cream sauce and crab, pasta primavera and eggplant or mushroom pasticcio, all available for a per pound price. They also offer main courses like chicken scaloppine, poached salmon with cucumber dill sauce, bal-

samic chicken and roasted peppers, as well as side dishes like tomato and fresh mozzarella salsa; roasted peppers, capers and eggplant; Caesar salad and various stuffed vegetables. These must be ordered in advance, but they always have a selection of pasta salads available in the store.

Their dessert selection usually includes cassata, a Sicilian chocolate cake made with pound cake, cream, fruit and chocolate; brownies, and tiramisu. This is a wonderful place to pick up dinner when you don't want to cook.

For fresh pasta, see also: Belfiore's, The Cheese Company, Cosolo's, Fratelli's, Mancinelli's and some Italian delis.

PASTA TRIVIA

1. Pasta was eaten first in China, but was only eaten by the lower classes. Noodles were a staple food during the Shang Dynasty (around 1700 B.C.). The Chinese have recorded eating noodles as early as 5,000 B.C.

2. The legend that the explorer Marco Polo brought noodles back to Italy from China may be true. However, pasta was already being eaten in Italy at that time (13th century).

3. The pasta of ancient Rome was made by baking kneaded flour and water mixture on large, porous, hot stones.

4. A wealthy nobleman from Palermo is supposed to have named macaroni. When his cook served him tube pasta, the nobleman exclaimed, "Cari! Ma cari! Ma caroni!" which means, loosely translated, "The dears! My dears! My precious darlings!"

5. In the Decameron (1350), Boccaccio describes the imaginary country of Bengodi, a land of mountains of grated Parmesan cheese on top of which workers make macaroni and ravioli and toss them down the hillsides to the hungry hordes below.

6. Pasta was first commercially exported in 1772–from Genoa to London .

7. A basket of dried pasta was a bequest in a 13th century Italian will.

8. Nineteenth century Englishmen thought noodles were food only good for children.

9. A dish called "Love in Disguise" was served in nineteenth century France. It was a stuffed calf's heart covered with a ground meat mixture, rolled in vermicelli and baked.

10. When Thomas Jefferson returned to the U.S. after being Ambassador to France, he ordered French macaroni and an Italian a pasta machine to be sent to him in the U.S.

11. There is a spaghetti museum in northern Italy at Pontedassio (near the Ligurian coast).

Specialty Meats

Dale's Exotic Game Meats

1961 W. 64th Avenue 657-9453
Monday–Friday, 7 am–4 pm. Closed Saturday & Sunday.

If you're looking for exotic meats, like alligator, rattlesnake or snapping turtle (bone-in or boneless!) Dale's is the place. It's a little hard to find, but the entrance is just to the north of Smokey's Barbecue on the north side of West 64th Avenue. Dale's is mostly wholesale, supplying restaurants with exotic meats from around the world, but they do a small retail business and are extremely pleasant and knowledgeable –and they're interested in sharing their expertise.

Thirty years ago, Dale took over his father's custom slaughtering business, and Dale's Beef & Buffalo was born. The buffalo was so successful that Dale began to deal exclusively with game meats. Now Dale's Exotic Game Meats is one of the largest suppliers of exotic meats in the country, supplying restaurants and retailers with rattlesnake, alligator, pheasant, elk and other farm-raised exotic meats, making their own game sausage and their own hot and sweet mustards to go with them. Dale now runs the canning plant, and has great gift packages of canned meats and soups, as well as stews and Dale's Wild West Chili with beans. The exotic meats side of the business is run by Bill Rowe and Paul Beier (son of Dale). This place is a great place to go for the exotic and the unexpected!

Fred's Fine Meats

5614 E. Cedar 377-2979
Monday–Saturday, 7 am–7 pm; Sunday, 8:30 am–5 pm.

Fred's been in the neighborhood 18 years, and offers dry-aged beef and lamb, homemade sausage and specialty items like frozen capons, duck and rabbit. Between the three of them, Fred, Clyde and John have about 130 years' experience in cutting, ageing and cooking meat. They always have a couple of kinds of fresh fish and also have barbecued baby back ribs and roast beef, cooked and ready to take home. Their meats are all top quality, and they will cut or cook any meat to suit your fancy. This is an old-fashioned butcher's shop with great products and service.

Oliver's Meat Market

1312 E. 6th Avenue 733-4629
Monday–Friday, 8 am–8 pm; Saturday, 8 am–7 pm;
Sunday, 9 am–6 pm.

Oliver's Meat Market is celebrating its 70th anniversary this year. It was started by Ed Oliver, grandfather of the present owner, Barry Oliver, in 1923. They cut all their own chops and steaks, and make their own sausage, including turkey and buffalo brats and Cajun sausage. They also roast their own beef and turkey breast. I once bought a large roast beef for a party from Oliver's. I roasted it at home and then brought it back to them, and they sliced it wafer-thin for me to serve at the party. They still retain that level of service.

Their deli section contains pancetta, bologna, pastrami, maple-glazed ham and other good quality meats, many of them from Boar's Head, a well-known quality brand. Visit them at the same time as you visit Green's market. They share the same front door!

Wally's Quality Meats & Deli

12755 W. 32nd Avenue, Wheat Ridge 232-5660
Monday–Friday, 9 am–6 pm; Saturday, 8:30 am–5:30 pm. Closed Sunday.

Thea Weyher, owner of Wally's, insists that she's going to concentrate more on the fresh meats and less on the deli items in the future, but there are plenty of both in this little gem of a store tucked away right off

Youngfield and 32nd in Wheat Ridge. When I walk in, the smell of a roast beef that Thea has in the oven is enough to make me salivate and remember the days when I walked into my house and smelled cooking. (This hasn't happened to me more than 3 times since I reached adulthood!) Thea has clients from all over the state who order their meat from her, including some in Vail, Evergreen and even Grand Junction. Briskets, prime rib, fillets, boneless leg of lamb–the meat is perfect looking, and all of the best available quality.

There is also homemade sausage: Southern-style, chicken apple, veal brats, German, Polish, Italian, chorizo, and Sheboygan brats. You can find homemade spaghetti with meatballs, baked beans with bacon, macaroni salad, hams and smoked bacon made right here, and other delicious items too numerous to mention.

Thea focuses on good food, with the good old-fashioned taste of great ingredients, and easy fixings that her customers love. She makes her own barbecue sauce, and suggests recipes to help you make a memorable meal. Special preserves, like red currant and lingonberry, can bring out the best in a roast or chops. Thea wants to write a cookbook–if she ever has time. I think it would be a good one.

The Cheese Company

735 S. Colorado Boulevard 778-6522 Fax: 778-1088
Monday–Friday, 9:30 am–7 pm; Saturday, 9:30 am–6 pm. Closed Sunday.

One hundred and fifty varieties of imported cheese are available at this great cheese chop in the Belcaro Shopping Center. Parmesano Reggiano, a nice selection of French goat cheeses, soft-ripened cheeses like Camembert and Chaumes, triple cream cheeses like Brillat-Savarin and St. André–this store could make a name-dropper out of anyone! They have English cheeses too, like Stilton, Cotswold and Huntsman. For the holidays, they have more, like Caerphilly and Cheshire.

Their pâtés and mousses look delicious, as do their own fresh pastas, homemade, and with fabulous fillings, like cheese-filled tortellini, tomato goat cheese and artichoke ravioli, and pesto provolone. Look in the takeout case and there are wonderful takeout selections like chicken curry, pasta salads and other delicious goodies.

Als available are all kinds of mustards, like jalapeno gold, honeycup, and sweet fire mustard, crackers and breadsticks,

fresh pastas, muffin mixes and bread mixes–everything you need to make cheese into a meal, except wine.

This is a lovely store. If you like good cheese, indulge yourself!

About Denver's Markets...

The proliferation of ethnic markets in Denver is the inspiration for this book. Driving around town, stopping at a Thai grocery, a Mexican market, a gourmet specialty store, a Middle Eastern shop or an Italian market, I never cease to be amazed by the variety of fresh vegetables, sauces, spices, meats and fish available to us.

Each store has its specialties, and discovering them is a rare pleasure. Look in the Asian markets for fresh exotic fruits and vegetables like plantains, daikon and durian, and herbs like basil and Kaffir lime leaves, as well as soy sauce, chili sauces and sambals, curry pastes and cooking oils. The Greek market has wonderful honey, halvah, cheeses and stuffed grape leaves. The Italian markets and delis offer superior pasta, olive oils and vinegars, while the Indian and Middle Eastern markets have fabulous teas and coffees, chutneys and spices. Don't miss the Mexican salsas, tortillas and tamales, the British scones and marmalades, the German sausages and rye breads or the Russian smoked fish and marinated vegetables.

These are only some of the ingredients to be found in the various shops and markets. I'm in favor of crossover shopping as well as ethnic shopping, and loved seeing the Jamaican woman who rejoiced at finding plantains in a Thai market, and the South American cook who discovered annatto seeds in the Korean grocery. Sometimes I just buy ingredients and look for a recipe to use them in. It certainly makes my cooking more interesting!

Asian Markets

Asian Market

333 S. Federal 937-1431
Daily, 9 am – 8 pm.

Located in the Asian Center on South Federal, this market has a good supply of fresh vegetables–Thai eggplant, okra, daikon, taro root, fennel, baby bok choy and lots more! They have Lao guava paste, tins of assorted English-style biscuits (cookies to Americans!) from Indonesia, and canned exotic fruits like longans and lychees.

and a nice selection of teas.

There are lots of frozen fish and some fresh fish as well, including octopus and milk fish, which is a large fish eaten a lot in Indonesia. It has a delicate flavor and is often served stuffed with garlic, onion and tomatoes.

Here's where I find wonton

Something that catches my eye, which I've seen in a couple of other Asian markets, is "mock chicken" made of soy, and canned. Useful for the vegetarians among us! They have many of the other ingredients that I've encountered in other Oriental markets, including hoisin sauce, sambals, hot chili sauce

skins to make Chinese steamed dumplings (see recipe for jaozi on page 73), and they also have a large selection of oils and small tins of Thai curry: red, yellow and green. I also see frozen betel nuts, which are chewed with betel leaves as a stimulant. Interesting!

Denver Oriental Supermarket

10260 E. Colfax Avenue, Aurora 360-7444
Thursday–Tuesday, 9 am–9 pm. Closed Wednesday.

The front door to this large market on Colfax is kept locked. There's a parking lot behind the store and you need to enter through the back. The store has quite an extensive fresh deli case, with unusual items such as different kinds of salted and seasoned fish: salted yellow fish, salted cod,and salted oysters; seasoned pollock, squid, and seasoned fresh crab. They also have fresh fish–some of which are disconcertingly large, with the heads still on, as well as fresh meats, with such items as knee cap and pork belly, as well as the more familiar rib eye roasts and short ribs.

There are some drinks I haven't seen in any other market, such as ginseng drink from Korea in a bottle, a yoghurt flavored drink called Yogloo and a canned milk drink called Milkis. Teas included jasmine, green tea and instant ginger tea.

You can find the usual array of soy, oyster and plum sauces, and several kinds of sesame oil. Apple and rice vinegars are available and in the freezer case I find sweet red bean buns, steamed fish cakes, several different kinds of rice cakes and dried persimmons.

There are a lot of different dried mushrooms, dried taro stems, and many different kinds of dried seaweed.

The store has a good selection of dried red and mung beans, soy beans, black beans, and millet, as well as pearl, whole and pressed barley. I notice a lot of fresh vegetables, many of which are unfamiliar. There are many kinds of greens, radishes and some long thin leeks. I've seen these in a number of Asian markets.

The store is clean and attractive and some items are marked in English, but many are not. If you know what you're looking for, this store is a good place to visit and pick up some unusual Asian specialties.

Granada Super Market

1275 19th Street 295-0296
Monday–Saturday, 8:30 am–6 pm; Sunday, 10 am–5 pm.

Sakura Square is the Japanese business center in lower downtown, around Larimer and 19th, and that's where the Granada Super Market is located. It has

Japanese, Chinese, Indonesian and Dutch specialties, as well as a surprising number of regular American products. Upstairs is a very nice fish market, with fresh shrimp, tuna, halibut, salmon in a sake mash, homemade cocktail sauce, cooked octopus from Japan and shad roe and calamari steak. There are also some more exotic things–fish eggs, including salmon eggs, smelt eggs, and even flying fish eggs, all of which look, to my untutored eye, more like bait than dinner.

ish, pickled ginger and several kinds of seaweed and kelp. Surprisingly, the canned birds nest soup is made in England by Bender and Cassel. Sharks fin soup is also available, and there are a number of other products common to most of the Oriental markets, such as hoisin, plum and soy sauces.

The Indonesian specialties include sambal chili sauce, a kind of salsa, satay sauce and ketjap soy sauce. (Ketjap is supposedly where our words ketchup or catsup came from). There are also cans of coconut milk and Java coffee beans. Indonesian flavorings for sweet dishes include rose and pandan. Pandan comes from the aromatic screw pine tree, and its flavoring is used for sweets, pastries and custards. Dried coconut cream, preserved ginger in syrup and canned chicory are also available.

Dutch products include such items as butter cookies, rusks (crunchy cookies like a cross between toast and biscotti that in England are given exclusively to teething babies!), Dutch jams and Droste chocolates.

Sakura Square is a lovely Asian oasis in the middle of lower downtown, that includes restaurants as well as grocery and other specialty stores.

There are three or four kinds of Japanese rice vinegar, as well as yam threads, bamboo shoots, gingko nuts and shiitake mushrooms. Other Japanese specialties include Japanese horserad-

THAI RED CURRY WITH CHICKEN

(Jit Na–Bangchang, J's Noodles)

1 teaspoon dried Kaffir lime rind* (washed in cold water)
1/4 cup warm water
1/2 teaspoon coriander seeds
2 tablespoons lemon grass, bottom part only, diced*
1/2 tablespoon galangal root, sliced fine (Thai ginger) *
1/2 head of garlic, cloves cleaned and chopped
2 large shallotts, chopped
10 small red dried Thai chiles
1/2 teaspoon shrimp paste*
1/2 teaspoon salt

> *Can be found
> in Thai markets

1 can coconut milk*
Dash coconut sugar (or palm sugar) *
1 tablespoon fish sauce or to taste*

1 lb. boneless chicken, cut into pieces
1/4 cup bamboo strips
2 or 3 small green Thai eggplants, cut in pieces*
5 or 6 large, fresh basil leaves
3 Kaffir lime leaves*
1 or 2 jalapenos, chopped (if desired)

Soak Kaffir lime rind in 1/4 cup warm water. Brown coriander
seeds in a frying pan on the stove and then crush. Put them, with the
next 7 ingredients, including water, into the blender and blend till
smooth. Put spices into a large saucepan on the stove and add up to
1/2 cup coconut milk. Cook over very low heat 25 minutes, stirring
occasionally. Then add chicken, fish sauce, sugar and the rest of the
coconut milk. Cook until the meat is cooked through. Add eggplant,
lime leaves, Thai eggplant, bamboo shoots and cook till the eggplant
is tender (about 5 minutes). Serves 4.

Indochina Enterprises

1045 S. Federal 935-0400
Monday–Thursday, 8:50 am–7:30 pm;
Friday & Saturday, 8:30–8 pm; Sunday, 8:30 am–7:30 pm.

Lots of fresh vegetables here, including fresh plantain, taro root, Thai eggplant, lemon grass, fresh ginger and baby bok choy. Also an incredible number of different beverages, including many kinds of tea: wild ginseng tea, gun powder tea, dieter's special tea, persimmon leaf tea and many others. They have dried sea cucumbers, which are black and strange-looking and lots of herb candies and other sweets and snacks.

Their cashews are $3.95 a pound, which is quite a bargain, and they have preserved duck eggs, large cans of staples for Oriental cooking, like hoisin and soy sauces, black bean sauce in huge jars, bottles of sesame oil and then, right in the middle, bottles of Lucozade, a glucose drink we used to get in England! They have Café du Monde coffee, just like you buy at the French Market in New Orleans I am surprised and pleased to find fresh durian, a large, globular fruit with spines sticking out all over. It's a seasonal fruit with an intense tropical flavor (and a terrible smell!). It can also be found canned.

Oriental Market

1443 Chester, Aurora 366-0454
Monday & Tuesday, 9 am–8 pm; Thursday–Saturday, 9 am–8:30 pm;
Sunday, 9 am–7 pm. Closed Wednesday.

This grocery has a variety of Asian products, with an emphasis on Korean and Japanese. There are several kinds of kim chee and kim chee sauces. It's a small neighborhood grocery store, well-organized with a nice atmosphere. There are many kinds of frozen and dried fish, as well as some unusual kinds of fresh fish. One I see while I'm here is whole octopus. The variety of Asian greens and vegetables is extensive, but since they aren't labeled in English, it's hard to figure out what all of them are. I could pick out white radishes, spinach, some thin leeks that I've noticed in other Oriental groceries, Chinese cabbage, and taro root.

As usual in Asian markets, you can find a number of different kinds of dried beans–black beans, mung beans, red beans and others. Pearl and whole barley are here, as well as rice flour and malt flour (this last I haven't encountered anywhere else). There are also whole chestnuts and many kinds of dried mushrooms. Huge bags of red pepper catch my eye, as do the number of rice cakes and kinds of tofu in the refrigerator case. There are also many different forms of dried seaweed. This is a good place to find Asian specialties if you know what you're looking for or if you're willing to just try out some new and different things.

JAOZI

(from Cindy Stone, as relayed by the Yang family of Kunming, China)

1 pkg. jaozi skins (round, 3" diameter dumpling skins, Kwan Sang Noodle Company brand, if possible)
1/2 lb. ground pork
1 lb. Napa (Chinese) cabbage, finely chopped, excluding the tough white stems
2 teaspoons grated ginger root
1/2 bunch finely chopped green onions
1 tablespoon sesame oil
1 tablespoon light soy sauce

Finely chop the cabbage and let it sit in a bowl with 2 tablespoons salt for about 20 minutes. Then put it into a colander and run water over it to get rid of the salt and squeeze it as dry as possible. Mix together the rest of the ingredients and add the cabbage. Lay the jaozi skins down flat and fill with 1 to 1-1/2 tablespoons filling. Pull up sides and crimp, using water to run your finger round the edge to moisten first. Then pinch in center and pinch sides in. When they are all filled and crimped together so they don't leak, cook in a steamer basket about 10 minutes or until cooked. Serve hot with jaozi sauce.

JAOZI SAUCE

1/4 cup light soy sauce
1/4 cup mild rice vinegar
2 dashes hot pepper oil
2 teaspoons sesame oil
2 teaspoons sugar
Green onion pieces to snip on top for garnish

Mix all dipping ingredients together in a jar and shake well. Serve as a dipping sauce for jaozi.

Laotian Oriental Food Store

7141 Irving, Westminster 428-3694
Monday–Saturday, 10 am–7 pm; Sunday, 10 am–6 pm.

This grocery store has been open for two years, run by Siphai and Sisopha, a shy but delightful couple. They cater mostly to a Thai and Laotian community. They have huge bags of rice, and also bowls and woks, candles and bags of bay leaves. There is Thai satay seasoning and cans of the different Thai curries–red, yellow, green and musaman (a corruption of Moslem). There are cans of fried squid, sliced baby ginger, green mustard pickles and many different cans of fish, like mackerel and sardines.

The selection of different kinds of noodles is good, and there are many packages of rice sticks and vermicelli. There is also a fine selection of fish and soy sauces. There are packets of Golden Bell curries, which usually come in hot or mild, and actually make reasonably good

curry for a mix.

The tins of fruit are fascinating, and there are many unfamiliar ones: mangosteen, rattan fruit, sapota and soursak in syrup, as well as something called rambutan, are side by side with the more familiar mangos in syrup and lychees.

I was surprised to find cookies from Holland and Horlicks, that milky bedtime drink beloved of English mothers. There is also a selection of syrups for making drinks or desserts, including rose, mali, cream soda and, surprisingly once again, Ribena, a blackcurrant syrup that is absolutely heavenly diluted with hot or cold water for a refreshing drink or poured neat over ice cream for the best ever blackcurrant sundae!

Lek's Asian Market

112 Del Mar Circle, Aurora, 366-2429
Daily, 10 am–6 pm.

Lek's Market is wonderful, partly due to the happy and helpful nature of Lek herself. She's never too busy to give advice about which kind of product to buy, or how to cook something, even when she's

surrounded by a group of women all talking away in Thai, or explaining to someone who doesn't understand English how American money works!

The store is very clean and bright, and offers a wonderful

variety of exotic produce, teas and coffees, canned goods and more! It was Lek who first persuaded me to try Thai coffee, very inexpensive and actually a mix of coffee and grain. Make it like regular coffee, but serve it with condensed milk, hot or iced. Fabulous! They also have Café du Monde coffee with chicory and Thai tea (loose tea with vanilla) and–would you believe–Ovaltine, another of those English bedtime drinks.

I'm intrigued by preserved or pickled mudfish (it looks like mud in a jar, actually–but I speak from total ignorance, so perhaps it's very tasty!). When I look it up in an encyclopedia of Asian cooking, I find out that it's considered a delicacy in the Philippines, pickled and usually served sautéed with tomatoes, onions and garlic. I always buy Kaffir lime leaves here: they're like bay leaves, but with a won-

derful lime flavor and fabulous in curry. I also recently tried miniature bananas from Ecuador! They're very good, with a slightly mushier texture than regular bananas, but an excellent flavor.Last fall I was fascinated to find something that was about the size of a small dinner plate, decorated with silk flowers and with incense in the middle–a sort of altar? I asked Lek and she patiently explained that in the November full moon the Thai people hold a special ceremony with this object, lighting the incense and blowing away all their grudges and bad thoughts, clearing their psychic or spiritual canvas for the year. It was such a charming idea that I bought one and used it as a centerpiece for several months.

Midopa Market

10700 E. Iliff, Aurora 369-9721
Thursday–Tuesday, 9 am–9 pm. Closed Wednesday.

Soy bean paste, hot bean paste and large bags of hot red pepper, both ground and powdered, are abundant at this market, which specializes in Korean, Japanese and Lao foods. There are many kinds of seaweed, huge bags of dried mushrooms, daikon, both fresh and pickled, and kim chee. They make their own kim chee here, so it might be worth trying.

Coconut milk, large bags of rice, and tempura batter are available too, but what really catches my eye is the sushi and something else called chop che, in plastic covered trays by the cash register, ready to take out.

I try the chop che, which turns out to be translucent vermicelli noodles, beautifully seasoned with sesame and spices, with pieces of fresh-cooked spinach. It's really good.

A few fresh vegetables are available, and there are two or three kinds of sesame oil, but the take-out is really the find in this place.

KOREAN BARBECUED BEEF

(Barbara Wright)

2 lbs. sirloin steak
4 scallions
5 cloves garlic
6 Tablespoons soy sauce
2 Tablespoons sesame oil
1/4 cup sugar
3 tablespoons sherry
1/4 cup beef stock
Fresh ground black pepper to taste

Slice sirloin very thinly against the grain. (It helps to put the steak into the freezer for 1/2 hour–1 hour before slicing.) Chop scallions and crush garlic or chop fine. Combine with other marinade seasonings in a large bow. Marinate at last 4 hours, preferably overnight. Grill on barbecue or broil quickly. Serve over rice.

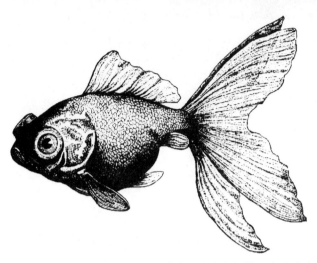

MARINATED FISH WITH BELL PEPPERS

Marinade:
1 lb. any firm, white fish like sole or snapper
3 tablespoons soy sauce
3 tablespoons key lime juice
1 tablespoon fish sauce
1 tablespoon galangal (Thai ginger), finely grated
4 Kaffir lime leaves
1 tablespoon soy oil
2 cloves garlic, pressed
1 teaspoon Chinese red chili sauce
1 tablespoon hoisin sauce
3 tablespoons white wine

Sliced strips of red, green and yellow peppers and red onions
2 tablespoons olive oil

Cooked rice

*Mix together all marinade ingredients except fish, in a glass or
ceramic dish. Cut fish into two or three pieces and marinate in the
refrigerator, preferably overnight. Turn the fish a few times. Discard
marinade and broil fish until it's flaky, 5–8 minutes. While fish is
cooking, sauté peppers and onions in olive oil. Serve over rice with
fish. Serves 2.*

ASIAN INGREDIENTS

Agar agar: *A gelatin made from seaweed. Used instead of gelatin in hot countries because it doesn't need to be cool to gel. I've also seen this sold in cans in Asian markets as grass jelly.*

Bean Curd or Tofu: *A cream-colored gel made from dried soybeans. Dried soybeans are soaked, puréed and boiled in water. The liquid is strained and mixed with a coagulant or solidifier which makes it form curds. These are compressed into bean curd.*

Bok Choy: *A kind of cabbage with thick, fleshy white stems and green leaves shaped rather like spinach. Both leaves and stems can be eaten. Bok choy is best when it's young, and then it's known as baby bok choy.*

Coconut Milk: *In many Asian countries, milk and cheese are not used at all, so coconut milk replaces it in desserts, is used to make cooling drinks and to cool the hot spices used in curries. Coconut milk tends to curdle if it is overcooked, so add it towards the end of cooking and stir with a ladle, lifting and pouring the milk to prevent boiling. Coconut milk can be made by squeezing fresh, grated coconut to extract the milk. However, canned coconut milk is available in many Asian markets.*

Fish Sauce: *A strongly flavored, pungent sauce used in Southeast Asia in much the same way as soy sauce*

Galangal or Thai ginger: *This spice has a hot peppery taste that could be described as a cross between horseradish and ginger. It's used in hot chili sauces and Thai curries. Known in Europe as galingale, it was long thought to be an aphrodisiac.*

Lemon Grass: *A major ingredient in Thai, Indonesian and Malaysian cooking, lemon grass is a fragrant grass with a white bulb and long, green leaves. It can be used by chopping the white part finely or crushing the whole plant to release the lemon flavor and taking it out of the dish before serving.*

Napa Cabbage or Chinese Cabbage: *This looks a little like romaine, a large, pale green cabbage with tightly packed leaves and a definite yet mild flavor. It's often stir-fried.*

Sambals: *Malaysian or Indonesian side dishes served with meals to complement flavors. Used in ways similar to Mexican salsas or*

Indian chutneys, they are often spicy and can be raw or cooked.

Satay: *Indonesian, Thai or Malaysian dish of skewered seasoned meat, poultry or seafood grilled over a charcoal fire and served with a dipping sauce. Sauces can be peanut-based or made with sweet soy sauce. This could be seen as an equivalent to our barbecue.*

Sichuan peppercorns: *These are not true peppercorns, but the aromatic red-brown seeds of the prickly ash tree. They have a peppery, lemon flavor.*

Soy Sauce: *Soy sauce has been used in China for over 3,000 years. Made from fermented soybeans, mixed with roasted grain and then fermented.*

Tamarind: *Fruit of the tamarind tree found in India, Indonesia and Malaysia, tamarind has a distinct, sweet-tart flavor. Used in curries, braised dishes and sauces to give a sharp flavor. Usually found in blocks with seeds or as a concentrate, it can also be used to make a refreshing drink.*

Mekong

1076 S. Federal, 937-7271
Daily, 9 am – 8 pm.

Walking into this Asian market and deli seems at first more like walking into a department store, because there's a counter with watches and jewelry right by the entrance. There's also an aisle of china and kitchen utensils. However, it's also a real grocery store with tins of English-style biscuits (cookies) and huge bags of rice, a whole aisle of spices, including annatto seed, as well as more common spices, some fresh vegetables, a meat and seafood counter (I see pork uteri at the meat counter but I haven't summoned up the courage to figure out how to cook them yet!)

There are many kinds of rice sticks and different noodles, and a whole deli section, with dumplings, roast pork, chewy rice in banana leaves and what I think are short ribs. I take home the short ribs and some rice, colored yellow, and they are delicious. I also try a tray of small, sausage-like patties, each with a hot pepper laid over the top. The design of the patties inside the package seduced me – and the taste was spicy and complex. This may be the only Asian deli in town.

Oriental Grocery Store

2965 W. 72nd Avenue, Westminster 430-4582
Daily, 9 am–8 pm.

This bright little market is run by an energetic Vietnamese woman named, in true melting-pot fashion, Chan O'Neill. She has lots of advice on how to use her products, especially the large array of fresh vegetables and herbs, like watercress and basil, that are less expensive here than in most supermarkets. Chan doesn't always know what all these greens are called, but she can tell you how to use them and what they'll taste good with. When I'm there she has leaves that can be stuffed like grape leaves, mint, sweet basil and snow peas, to name a few.

Chan carries an enormous selection of noodles, including rice noodles, spring roll skins, cans of bamboo shoots and small tins of various Thai curries, hoisin sauce, plum sauce, different kinds of soy sauce,as well as things I've never heard of, like powdered sushi and banana blossoms in brine. I'm interested to see that she has satay sauce mix, for making Thai satay, a great appetizer that can be made with beef, pork or chicken and usually has a wonderful peanut dipping sauce. She also has annatto seeds, which I've only ever found in one or two places in Denver. One thing that sounds intriguing is coconut cream powder. Since canned coconut milk will only keep for a few days in the fridge after opening, perhaps coconut cream powder could be reconstituted a little at a time, with less waste?

Chan says that the people shop who shop here are Lao, Thai, all kinds of Oriental. She asserts that Oriental people stay slender by eating mostly rice and vegetables instead of a lot of meat. With the wonderful selection of fresh vegetables here, that wouldn't be a hardship!

Oriental Grocery Market

11700 Montview 343-9450
Daily, 10 am–6 pm.

This market is owned by a cheerful and friendly man by the name of Phon Techapaikaweekul. (He warned me his last name was very long, but he had to spell it for me to believe him!) His English is good, and he's very knowledgeable about the different kinds of vegetables he carries. When I'm there, he has fresh ginger, dill, mint, fresh coconut and winter melon, several kinds of squash and 3 or 4 different kinds of basil. His produce is seasonal to some extent, and fresh vegetables and fruit arrive late Wednesday and all day Thursday, so that's probably the best time to shop for the many wonderful and unusual items. I am surprised and delighted to find fresh Thai eggplant, which is small, and even baby Thai eggplant, which is really miniscule, as well as galangal (Thai ginger) and okra, chayote, a kind of watercress I've never seen before and fresh pennyroyal leaves!

Other treasures include many kinds of soy sauce, fish sauce, oyster sauce and rice vinegar, as well as chili and sesame oil and satay sauce mix. Like most of the Thai grocers, Phon has large bags of rice and a selection of Oriental noodles. But I also find some wonderfully unusual and sometimes puzzling ingredients, like a candy called Coffee Go for 89¢ – for when you don't have time to drink your cup of coffee, dried betel leaves like those used fresh to make the Indian pan–the wonderful little package of seeds and flavors we'd get after eating in Indian restaurants in London.

Purple yam jam looks interesting, and so do dried lily flowers and cans of lotus root and Thai jelly glass. Small cans of Thai curry–red, yellow and masaman–I've tried these and they're just great with some coconut milk and a couple of Kaffir lime leaves, cooked with perhaps a few tablespoons of peanut butter and then poured over rice sticks or angel hair noodles for a great vegetarian curry.

By Western standards, the shop is rather dark and disorganized, but it contains some real treasures. Phon promises he's getting in more cookbooks that explain Thai cooking in English and Thai. I'll be going back for one!

Pacific Mercantile

1925 Lawrence   295-0293
Monday–Saturday, 8 am–6 pm; Sunday, 9 am–2 pm.

Located on the corner of Sakura Square, this market has a good selection of fresh fish: flounder, mackerel, perch, catfish, tuna and yellowtail tuna, sea bass and snapper. They also have quail eggs, which are quite beautiful sitting in their tiny cardboard box of a dozen. I'm told that they taste just like chicken's eggs, but of course they look so tiny and delicate, they'd make any dish look exotic. They're often used in sushi.

The vegetables at Pacific Mercantile are also attractive

and exotic, with shiitake and enoki mushrooms, daikon sprouts and daikon and taro root, and lots of nice fresh greens. There's also a fine selection of teas–all green, and herbs and spices.

There are many kinds of canned fish, including whelks, sardines, mackerel, anchovies and tuna fillets. Dipping sauces abound, from Indonesian sambals to Thai satay sauces, many kinds of hot chili pastes and sauces, and soy and fish sauces.

There are also many kinds of soy, tamari and yakitori (barbecue) sauces and ketjap manis, which is a sauce used in Javanese cooking, made from palm syrup, garlic, star anise and Thai ginger, also known as galangal.

There's a whole section of the store devoted to ceramics and rice cookers. This store has a whole range of Asian products, from Thai curries to kim chee to many kinds of seaweed.

Seoul Oriental Market

6150 N. Federal 650-0101
Monday–Saturday, 9 am–8 pm; Sunday, 10 am–7 pm.
Closed Wednesday.

You could easily miss this market if you didn't know where to look for it–it's right off Federal on the west side of the street, hidden behind a car wash. It's basically a Korean grocery store, with a 70-80% Korean clientele, but they have some other Asian specialty foods as well.

Mr. Chang Kung O, who owns this store with his wife Kyong O, is full of information, and offers some insights about the difference between Western and Korean eating habits. The Korean diet is founded on rice and kim chee (kimchi). Kim chee is a hot and spicy fermented pickle, made most often from napa cabbage, but sometimes from other vegetables like radish or green onion, and seasoned with chiles, salt and garlic.

It's an acquired taste, as it's very spicy and has a very pungent smell. (Mr. O warned me not to smell the kim chee before I ate it, as it might put me off!) It's served as a side dish with almost every Korean meal, and sometimes used in cooking as well, to flavor soups and stews. Red chile powder is also an important ingredient in Korean food and here they have a lot of it, ground coarse or fine. There are several varieties of the equally important bean paste: fermented black, a hot bean paste and a soy bean paste, as well as hot pepper paste.

I find many different kinds of tea, some familiar, like Darjeeling and green tea, and some less so, such as roasted barley tea. There's also Oriental iced tea and something called pearl barley beverage. Mr. O has a good selection of soy sauces, rice cooking wine and rice vinegars. There are several kinds of dried seaweed, lots of dried mushrooms and dried fish, including anchovies. I take a jar of kim chee, one of the many varieties available, and the one Mr. O judges most suitable for a kim chee novice.

BEEF SATAY

2 lbs. boneless beef, cut into 1" cubes
Marinade: 4 tablespoons soy sauce
3 teaspoons lime juice
2 tablespoons oil
1 clove garlic
1/2" fresh ginger, grated

2 tablespoons oil for sautéing

1 tablespoon coriander seed
1 large red chile
1 tsp. turmeric
1" fresh ginger, chopped
1/2 medium red onion, coarsely chopped

1 cup coconut milk
4 tablespoons peanut butter

2 tablespoons grated lemon peel
3 tablespoons soy sauce
3 tablespoons lemon juice
2 tablespoons sugar

Marinate meat in marinade overnight. Drain and discard marinade. Heat 2 tablespoons. oil in skillet. Sauté meat slowly, together with coriander seed, chopped red chile, turmeric, ginger and onion. Add coconut milk, peanut butter, lemon peel, soy sauce, lemon juice and sugar. Cook slowly 20 minutes. Do not boil. Remove from heat and serve over rice.

Tan Phat Oriental Market

1001 S. Federal 935-3766
Daily, 9 am–7 pm.

One whole wall has huge bags of rice piled against it, so high I wonder if I could be totally buried if they all came falling down! This store has a huge selection of different sauces and vinegars: rice vinegar, teriyaki, stir fry sauce, spare rib sauce, sesame paste and many, many others. They have curry gravy from Singapore, fried garlic, coconut milk, and cans of sugar cane and soursop in syrup. This market carries goods from all over Asia: from Indonesia, Laos, China, Vietnam and Thailand.

They have fresh Kaffir lime leaves, which I haven't come across anywhere else except at Lek's Thai market before, but which are wonderful in curries. There's also a variety of dry goods, such as hats from Vietnam, underwear (including some rather serviceable-looking white cotton bras—Frederick's of Hollywood they're not!) from Taiwan, little packages of desserts like sweet rice and beans. They also sell bowls, plates and ricemakers. Most intriguing to me are the paper plates with rice cake on them, which you can buy and top with your sauce of choice to eat here or take out.

Patronize this market and you can count on being treated with helpfulness and good humor.

Thai Bin Duong / Pacific Ocean Marketplace

375 S. Federal 935-2470
Daily, 9 am – 8 pm.

Located in the Asian Center on South Federal Boulevard, this market seems very much like a regular supermarket—until you look at what's on the shelves! Like most of the Asian markets, they have a wide selection of teas, dried mushrooms, different kinds of flour, like rice flour, tapioca flour and potato starch, and many different kinds of Oriental noodles.

They also have quite a selection of Eastern medicinal remedies, like royal jelly and pollen extract from China. And, for those who are looking for long life and happiness – instantly – there's instant ginseng tea! There is also a fine selection of labor-saving mixes, like instant curry mixes, roast duck spices, kim chee mix and Knorr soups. Their line of candies is extensive, and includes such items as dried ginger candy, tamarind candy and love prune candy, an unlikely mixture in my book, since, according to the label, it's made with prunes, licorice, sugar and salt.

Their canned goods are similar to those in most of the Asian markets: lychees, pineapple, jackfruit, but they also have canned baby bananas. And their selection of drinks in the refrigerator case is surprising: grass jelly, mung bean with coconut, tofu soy drink, basil seed and many more! The basil seed drink has the consistency of runny tapioca, which is rather strange to the Western palate.They also have little miniature custard-like puddings, frozen fish and grated cassava. The meat and fish market is quite astonishing to Western eyes. Where else would you see pork stomachs, ducks' feet, pork hearts or salmon heads?

The vegetables are labeled in English, so I can tell that there's fresh taro root, water chestnuts, cassava, lotus root and fresh oyster mushrooms. This might be a good starting place for the novice shopper for Asian foods, exotic without being too startling!

SICHUAN PEPPER CHICKEN
(Cindy Stone)

1 lb. boneless chicken breast, cut into small pieces
2 tablespoons cornstarch
1 tablespoon soy sauce
1/4 cup vegetable oil
10–12 Sichuan red peppercorns
1 teaspoon fresh grated ginger

Marinate chicken in the cornstarch and soy sauce for 30 minutes or more. Discard marinade. Stir fry chicken in the vegetable oil until just cooked. Pour out any excess oil, leaving about 1 Tablespoon. Add the Sichuan peppers and brown in the oil. Add the fresh grated ginger. Then add the following sauce and cook until just warm. Serve sprinkled with green onions.

SAUCE

1 tablespoon sherry
1 tablespoon cornstarch
1 tablespoon sesame oil
2 tablespoons soy sauce
1/2 teaspoon sugar
Dash hot chili oil
Chopped green onions for garnish

Mix the preceding ingredients and put into the wok. Serve sprinkled with green onion tops, finely chopped.

Xuan Trang

1095 S. Federal 936-7537
Daily, 9 am – 8 pm.

The first thing I notice when I walk into this market is the variety of flavoring essences: things like mali, ourian, and pandan, that I've never heard of. I look them up and find that mali is jasmine, and pandan is an essence made with the leaves of the pandan or screw pine tree. These essences are used in flavoring sweets in Thai and Indonesian cooking. This store has lots of candies and cookies, including cream-filled love rolls (could they possibly be as good as specialties like Horlicks and Ovaltine (those bed-time drinks from jolly old England!) Café du Monde ground coffee with chicory, and ground espresso coffee. Lemon grass powder and dried galangal (Thai ginger) are available and so is dried bamboo. In the back of the store is a large selection of tea sets, candles and altars, bead curtains, knives and cleavers, and, surprisingly, colanders in various sizes and a selection of bright colors–pink, purple and blue. I am particular-

they sound?) and specialties such as preserved Sichuan vegetables, dried salt lime, many kind of soy sauce, pickled cassia leaves and tamarind with honey.

There are also some European ly taken with a small brown tea set, consisting of a small pot and four little cups.

Visit Xuan Trang and pick up some dishes and home furnishings as well as food.

British Markets

Canos Collection

235 Fillmore 322-0654
Monday–Saturday, 10:30 am–5:30 pm. Closed Sunday.

This little gift shop cum teashop cum British cum South American specialty store is certainly one-of-a-kind! It's run by a Welshwoman, and they have some Welsh specialties in the store. Welsh kissing spoons are wooden spoons carved out of wood, supposedly for men to give their sweethearts. They also have Welsh cakes, which my mother used to make for my Welsh father, and they're good, though not at all like my mother's recipe! They also have scones and the usual kinds of British specialties–digestive biscuits, scone mixes, teas, jams and sometimes fresh scones to take home, which I certainly like. They have British aprons and tea cosies and china. There is also a primitive Mexican and South American theme, and they carry gift items from those areas.

The English Teacup

1930 S. Havana, Aurora 751-3052
Monday–Friday, 10 am–5:30 pm; Saturday, 10 am–5 pm.
Closed Sunday.

This was like a trip back into my past, with all the products and brand names I grew up with in England: Bird's custard, Marmite and Bovril, two yeast-extract like spreads that only English and Australian people love, Weetabix cereal, Yorkshire pudding (although we didn't make it from a mix), pickled onions (heavenly with a hearty English cheese, but don't eat them before a date, like I always did–they don't add to your sex appeal!)

English tea is available in several varieties, the best known of which are Typhoo (their advertising slogan-Yoo-hoo! Typhoo! - meaning "Tea's ready!") and PG Tips ("Tea you can really taste!" –and always advertised by a family of chimpanzees dressed up in Sunday-best clothes and having a tea party–hardly an American's idea of a decorous English afternoon tea.) And of course to go with the tea is Walker's shortbread and even some scones! And to put on the scones, a little English jam–delicious! There are also steak and kidney pies, English pork or beef sausages, Cornish pasties, even sausage rolls. Oh, and don't forget the malt vinegar–perfect for those authentic British fish and chips, wrapped in greasy newspaper.

For those who still hanker for nursery foods there is blanc-mange mix, a kind of bland-tasting pudding, and tinned rice and sago puddings. Reminds me of the A.A. Milne poem (he's the creator of Winnie the Pooh)

What is the matter with Mary Jane?

She's perfectly well and she hasn't a pain

And it's lovely **rice pudding** for dinner again

What **is** the matter with Mary Jane?

Jeanne Fox, the owner of this elegant little shop, also has a lovely collection of English tea pots, china, Toby jugs and even china cheese dishes for sale. All you Anglophiles, make tracks!

Presidential Food Facts

When the King and Queen of England visited Franklin D. Roosevelt, he served them hot dogs.

House of Windsor

1050 S. Wadsworth, Lakewood 936-9029
Monday–Friday, 10 am–5:30 pm; Saturday, 10 am–4:30 pm.
Closed Sunday.

A shopping center on South Wadsworth and Mississippi is an unlikely location for an authentic British teashop, but that's where you'll find the House of Windsor. They have a fine selection of pork pies, pasties, sausage rolls, scones, cakes and shortbread. They also have other authentic British items like steak and kidney pies, English sausages (pork or beef), wonderful English cheeses like Cheshire, Stilton and Cotswold, and kip-pers–once a breakfast staple when I grew up in England, but now largely relegated to the pages of British mysteries.

Derek and Brenda Williams run the House of Windsor, where you can sit and have a civilized pot of tea with lunch or at teatime. Four o'clock is considered the correct hour for tea, although of course English people can manage a cup of tea anytime. The walls are lined with beautiful china cups and teapots, reminders of a more leisurely time, when everything stopped for tea. In England, at least where I come from, it still does. My mother doesn't believe there's anything that can't be cured by either a good cup of tea or running it under the cold tap!

Don't forget to pick up some of the English specialties to take home with you—like Fortnum and Mason tea, or Robertson's lemon curd (delightful on one of those scones!) or one of several kinds of lemon, orange or grapefruit marmalade. There are also British-style pickles, which are actually more like what we call chutney (Branston is one of the most famous brands). They're great with sharp cheese and crackers or toast. A couple of other items I remember from my youth were also there—Ambrosia creamed rice pudding and several kinds of brown sauce, which are also served with cheese.

For an authentic touch of British hospitality, you can't go wrong at the House of Windsor. It's jolly good!

THE STORY OF TEA

Tea is drunk by more people around the world than any other beverage except water. Legend tells that tea was discovered accidentally by the Chinese Emperor Shen Nung. The emperor was drinking hot water in the shade of a tree when a tea leaf floated into his cup. This was around 2740 B.C., and thereafter tea leaves were dried, powdered and mixed into hot water. During the Ming Dynasty, 1368–1644 A.D., tea leaves began to be brewed the way we brew them today.

Tea was introduced to Japan by Buddhist priests and brought from Japan to Europe by the Dutch in the early seventeenth century. It was too expensive to be drunk by the majority of people until the late eighteenth century.
In the United States, tea was the favorite drink until the Boston Tea Party of 1773, when tons of tea were thrown into Boston Harbor in protest against taxation by the British.

Iced tea was invented in the U.S. in 1901, when a tea salesman at the World's Fair in St. Louis helped his customers beat the heat by pouring his tea over ice. Iced tea has been the most popular form of tea in the U.S. ever since. The tea bag was also invented in the U.S. A tea salesman began sending out tea samples in little silk bags. His customers thought that they were premeasured tea and brewed them in the bags, and finding them so convenient, they ordered more!

KINDS OF TEA

There are three basic kinds of tea: black tea, which includes almost all Indian tea, green tea, which includes almost all Japanese tea, and oolong, which has some of the characteristics of each.

Black tea *is dried, rolled to bruise the leaves and release the flavor and fermented to develop the fragrance of the leaves. The fermentation is then stopped by firing—exposing the tea to a blast of hot, dry air.*

Green tea *is not fermented, but is steamed, rolled and fired. The leaves remain green.*

Oolong *is partially fermented tea. It is sometimes mixed with jasmine or gardenia to make a scented tea.*

TO MAKE A GOOD POT OF BRITISH TEA

1. Bring a kettle of fresh, cold water to a rolling boil.

2. Warm the teapot by pouring in a little hot water, swishing it around and pouring it all out.

3. Put a teaspoon full of good quality tea for each person into the teapot, plus one for the pot.

4. Fill the pot with hot water and wait a few minutes for the tea to steep or "mash".

In England, black tea is served with milk and sugar. The milk is always put into the cup first, and the tea poured, sometimes through a strainer, into the cup onto the milk. Cream is not used in tea as it is in coffee because it changes the flavor of the tea.

German Markets

Black Forest Specialties

9436 W. 58th, Arvada 425-0265
Tuesday–Thursday, 9 am–5:30 pm; Friday, 9 am–6:30 pm;
Saturday, 9 am–3 pm. Closed Sunday & Monday.

It's a little hard to find this German-style market, since it doesn't face the street, but it's in the Arvada Plaza shopping Center at the corner of Independence and 58th Avenue. However, when you do find it, you'll be surprised by the selection of German specialties, including some things I haven't seen anywhere else. Ingrid, the owner, says that they cater to a number of European tastes, including German, Hungarian, Polish and Czech. There's a good selection of hams and sausages, as well as some herring and cheeses. The pickles are many and various, and there are also several kinds of flat and deli rye breads, as well as fresh ryes. A large and varied shelf or two is dedicated to Maggi soups and seasonings and another to all kinds of pudding mixes. There are also some Knorr soups.

There are seasoning mixes for sauerbraten and goulash, as well as many different kinds of syrup: blackcurrant, strawberry and raspberry. There's German-style coffee, tubes of mustard as well as mustards in jars, many herbal teas or tisanes and, of course, some creams and lotions from Germany as well.

Ingrid plans to concentrate more on the deli and sandwiches than the German specialties in the future, so call first to make sure she has what you're looking for.

CABBAGE POCKETS

(This recipe is from Tammy Davis, of Divine Temptations)

1 large head cabbage, chopped fine
2 medium onions, chopped fine
1-1/2 lbs. ground beef, 80% lean
1/2 teaspoon garlic powder
Salt and pepper to taste (recommended: 2 teaspoons black pepper)
Any bread or pizza dough

Cook cabbage in kettle in 1/3 cup water, with lid on for 1/2 hour. Meanwhile, sauté ground beef and onions. Salt and pepper to taste and add garlic powder. Roll out dough to 1/8" thick. Cut into 5" x 5" squares. Mix cabbage and ground beef together and place 1 big scoop filling in middle of each square. Pinch sides to top and top to bottom. Place pinched side down on greased pan (a cookie pan with a lip will do. Don't use a pan without a lip because juice will run out all over the oven!) Brush the tops with butter. Bake at 350° till brown, 1/2 hour to 45 minutes. Brush a little melted butter on top when they come out of the oven.

TAMMY'S CHEESE SPREAD

(Tammy Davis, Divine Temptations)

2 lbs. margarine, softened
5 oz shredded Swiss cheese
5 oz shredded Cheddar cheese
4 cloves garlic, minced fine
1 teaspoon sweet basil, dried (or 3 teaspoons fresh)

Blend all ingredients in a food processor. Spread on French bread and broil under broiler to melt. This spread will last in the fridge for a while and can be used for garlic bread or spread on flour tortillas, cut in fourths and broiled. When cool these become firm and crisp and can be eaten like chips—if they last that long!

Indian Food

The food of India is as varied and complex as the country itself, ranging from the aromatic and intricate flavors of the north, where the clay tandoor oven is used to bake meats and breads, to the pungent, spicy dishes of the south, where chilis are used to lend a fiery heat to stews and sauces. In between, many regional cuisines flourish. However, there are some things that Indian meals all have in common. A variety of dishes is usually served at once, rather than in courses as we tend to eat here in the West. Meat and chicken dishes, vegetables, at least one rice dish, or one or several kinds of bread, and one or more dals or lentil dishes are usually served at once, accompanied by chutneys, pickles and often a raita–a cooling salad made of cucumbers and onions with a yoghurt dressing.

Many snacks, like samosas, can be served as one dish among many put on the table at once, or as Western-style appetizers. (Samosas are deep-fried pastries filled with a mixture of potatoes and sometimes meat. They are delicious served with chutneys, the most usual being tamarind or mint.)

Indian curries are extremely diverse and can be very hot and spicy or sweet and aromatic. Indians don't use the curry powders we find in our supermarkets or even in some of the specialty stores. They usually mix their own masalas (masala simply means a ground spice mixture) because the freshly ground and mixed spices are tastier and more aromatic. The taste of ground spices seems to fade rather quickly, so if you buy a ground spice or curry mixture, it's better to use it within 3 months or so.

Indian sweets are traditionally eaten as snacks rather than as a dessert to follow the meal, but they are delicious, often fudge-like and made from milk, or halvah-like and made from vegetables or wheat. There is also kulfi, the delicious Indian version of ice cream, often flavored with mango or pistachio. I have seen mixes in the Indian markets from which to make some Indian desserts, but the ready-made ones they have in their refrigerator cases are so good that I haven't yet felt the need to try out the mixes!

INDIAN INGREDIENTS

Basmati: *Fragrant, expensive rice grown in the Dehradun region of India*

Besan: *Chickpea flour*

Biryani: *Festive dish made with rice and spiced meat or chicken*

Chana: *Chickpea (chana dal is a split chickpea pulse)*

Chapati: *Flat bread made with whole wheat flour*

Dal: *Pulse, lentil*

Garam: *Hot (garam marsala are hot spices)*

Kofta: *Meatball*

Korma: *Rich meat dish*

Kulfi: *Indian icecream often flavored with mango or pistachio*

Masala: *A mixture of spices used in Indian cooking. They are made by grinding whole spices into powder. Because ground spices lose their flavor quickly, they are usually made in fairly small quantities.*

Pan (paan): *Betel leaf; a collection of spices wrapped in a betel leaf and served after an Indian meal. These can be very elaborate, sometimes containing gold or silver leaf called vark.*

Papar or pappadum: *A wafer-like cracker or bread made from lentil, rice or potato flour. They are deep-fried and served as a snack, sometimes with chutneys.*

Paratha: *Layered, buttery Indian bread*

Poori: *Deep-fried Indian bread*

Raita: *Indian side dish made with yoghurt and a vegetable, often cucumber*

Samosa: *Pastries stuffed with meat and vegetables and deep-fried*

Tandoor: *Clay, beehive-shaped oven used for baking*

Usli ghee: *Clarified butter*

Vark: *Thin, edible silver or gold foil, used for garnishing desserts and rice*

Indian Markets

Kohinoor Indo-Pak Imports

3140 South Parker Road, Aurora 369-6884
Tuesday–Friday, 1:30 pm–9 pm, Saturday, 11 am–9 pm;
Sunday, 11 am–7 pm.

This Indian and Pakistani food store has lots of exotic-looking snacks. In the refrigerator case are turnovers called samosas already cooked and ready to heat up, and some desserts, though not so many as in the other Indian market. There are many masalas or spice mixes, including those for kheema (minced meat) chai (Indian spiced tea) and tandoori. Tandoori is the name given to food cooked in a tandoor oven, a beehive-shaped clay or mud oven that's heated with charcoal to a very high temperature. The food is put into the oven through a hole in the top.

There are dals and beans in tubs, to be sold in bulk and 25 lb. bags of rice. Garlic, prawn and ginger pickles and various kinds of chutney sit side-by-side with British custard mixes by Bird's and Brown and Polson. Corn flour and flaked rice are available, as well as fried vermi-

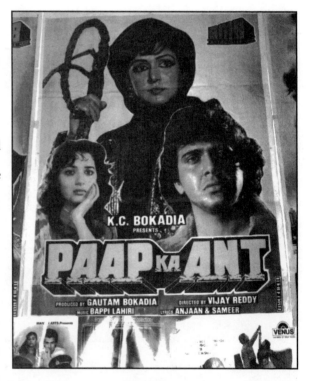

celli with milk–something I've never heard of. There are also mixes to make the Indian gulab julam or fudge-like desserts like those they have in the refrigerator case.

There are some interesting preserves, including rose petal flavor as well as the more usual orange marmalade. Plum and mango chutneys look good, and so do rose, mango and orange syrups. There are also English squashes. These are not a kind of gourd! In England, squash is a concentrate of orange, lemon or other fruit, to which water is added to make a non-carbonated summer drink.

The people in the store are very helpful and try to explain what various ingredients are and what they're used for. I am happy to find masalas for pan, which are the Indian spices, usually wrapped in a fresh betel leaf, used to end an Indian meal. The fresh betel leaf is not available in the U.S., although I did find some dried in the Oriental Grocery Market. The pan masala makes an authentic ending to an Indian meal, served in a little dish with a spoon for putting a little into your palm.

The hours for this store seem particularly variable, so be sure to call before you go.

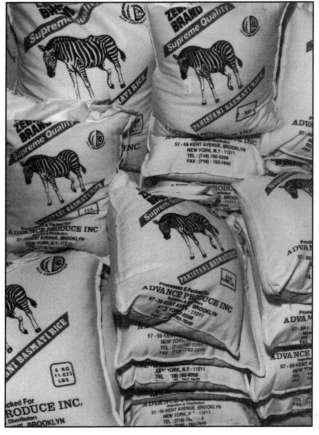

CURRY PASTES AND POWDERS

There are many different curry pastes and powders available in Asian, Indian and Middle Eastern markets. They vary from korma, which is spicy and aromatic, to vindaloo, which is incendiary and has a sour flavor from the addition of tamarind or vinegar that makes it go well with strongly flavored meats like duck or pork. In the Thai markets, you will come across little cans of red, green, yellow or mussaman curry. The green curry is based on green chiles and the red curry on red chiles. The yellow and mussaman curries are often milder, and get their color from the addition of turmeric. The red and green curry pastes can be used to make fiery curry sauces, and need the addition of coconut milk to cool them off enough that they don't set your entire mouth on fire.

Generally, the curry pastes keep their flavor longer than the dry ground spices. If you buy the little cans, they make just enough for a sauce to serve 4 people (see recipe below).

SHRIMP WITH GREEN CURRY SAUCE

1 can Thai green curry paste (4 oz.)
1 can coconut milk (13.4 oz.)
3–4 Kaffir lime leaves
1 lb. shrimp, cooked in boiling water until pink, drained and shelled, with veins removed
1 lb. rice sticks or angel hair noodles, cooked 3–5 minutes and drained

Heat curry paste gently with Kaffir lime leaves. Add coconut milk and mix thoroughly. Add cooked, shelled shrimp. Pour over drained noodles and return to pan to toss thoroughly. Serves 4 hungry people.

TANDOORI

A tandoor is a clay oven, shaped rather like a beehive with an opening in the top for putting the food in. Indian breads like naan can be stuck to the side of the tandoor and allowed to cook there. Tandoori chicken and sometimes fish are cooked in this oven, which has no temperature controls but which cooks whole pieces of chicken or fish or various kinds of kebabs beautifully by quickly searing the outside while leaving the interior moist.
Tandoori spices can be bought to make the tandoori chicken that is so often found in Indian and Pakistani restaurants. Don't worry if

your chicken isn't quite as orange as the chicken you eat in Indian restaurants. Theirs is often colored with an orange-red food coloring that's added to the chicken as it marinates.

Since most of us don't have a tandoor at home, we have to improvise, but I've found that quite respectable tandoori chicken can be made on the outdoor barbecue.

TANDOORI CHICKEN

4 chicken breasts, skinned
Tandoori spices (from Indian markets)
1/2 cup plain yoghurt
1 teaspoon lemon juice

Skin chicken breasts, but leave them on the bone. Mix 2–4 tablespoons tandoori spices (depending on how spicy you like your chicken) with the yoghurt and lemon juice. Marinate the chicken breasts in the mixture in the refrigerator overnight or for at least several hours, turning occasionally. Cook outdoors on the barbecue or under the broiler for about 15 minutes, turning once. Discard any leftover marinade.

SLOW-COOKED INDIAN POTATOES

5–6 medium potatoes
1 large clove elephant garlic, chopped fine
4 tablespoons vegetable oil
1/2 teaspoon ground asafetida
3 tablespoons ground cumin
1/2 teaspoon ground hot peppers
1 tablespoon turmeric
15 fl. oz. can tomato sauce

Wash and cut up potatoes into small pieces. This allows the fabulous sauce to penetrate into them from all sides! Heat the oil in a large casserole or heavy saucepan. Put in the asafetida, cumin and chopped elephant garlic. Stir and add the ground red peppers. Now put in the potatoes and turmeric. Stir. Let cook for about 4 minutes, stirring once in a while.

Add tomato sauce and 15 fl. oz. (1 tomato sauce can) water. Bring to the boil and turn heat down. Allow to simmer, covered, for about 1-1/2 hours. These potatoes are very good served with any meat dish, but especially with Indian dishes like tandoori chicken. Serves 4–6.

Tajmahal Imports

3095-C S. Peoria, Aurora 751-8571
Daily, 11 am – 8 pm. Closed Tuesday.

Surprisingly to me, since I had no idea of its existence, this store has been in the area for ten years. It's one of five Indian grocery stores scattered across the region with headquarters in Dallas. 90% of Tajmahal's customers are Indian or Pakastani, and they come there to find all the wonderful spicy condiments, chutneys and other exotic ingredients they need to make tasty and delicious Indian food. The store carries Indian tea, together with tea masala – the special spices you need to make the Indian tea or chai, with milk and sugar. It's a real treat, spicy and smooth. There's also a great selection of Indian snack foods and many kinds of dal – split peas, lentils, garbanzos (chana dal). The red lentils (actually, they're a beautiful salmon-color) are sometimes hard to find in regular markets. They had little brown lentils that I'd never seen anywhere else.

The selection of Indian breads is also very good: poori, chapati, and naan in the refrigerator case and pappadums in packages. (Pappadums look like a cross between a tortilla and a flat bread, but when cooked in hot oil they puff up and taste delicious.) I immediately became addicted to naan with coriander chutney on it. I also tried some canned creamed spinach with spices that went remarkably well with the naan and chutney. There's a selection of Indian spices, including cardamom seeds, and many different kinds of flour, like gram flour and moong dal flour, and even urad bean flour, which is used to make pappadums.

Best of all, in the refrigerator case at the front of the shop is a selection of desserts, most of them milk-based and tasting rather like very rich and fabulous fudge. Some are flour-based and taste more like halvah. Also, to my delight, there were samosas, one of the many Indian snacks you can buy from street vendors on the streets in most Indian cities – and in parts of London – just waiting to be taken home and crisped in the oven!

INDIAN BREADS

*There are many kinds of Indian breads, known collectively as roti. In the south, the bread is often made from rice and lentils and in the north from wheat. **Chapatis** are thin, flat, unleavened bread made from finely ground whole wheat flour. They are cooked on a heavy pan over a fire or on top of the stove. **Naan** is a soft, pita-like bread often cooked in a tandoor oven. Naans are sometimes stuffed with chicken or cheese or potato mixtures. **Pooris** are fried breads served with vegetarian dishes and sometimes stuffed like a sandwich with curries or potatoes for a snack. **Poppadums** are flat, dried crackers made from lentil, rice or potato flour. They are available in packages and should be fried in oil so that they puff up. They can then be eaten with chutneys, particularly with mint and tamarind chutneys.*

Naan and some of the other breads are available in Indian and Middle Eastern markets in the refrigerator case. They make great snack foods served with dips or chutneys, like Avocado Chile Dip or Coriander Chutney.

AVOCADO CHILE DIP

Two large tablespoons green chile chutney
1 large, ripe avocado
Naan, halved and heated in the toaster or toaster oven

Mix the chutney with the mashed avocado. Serve with naan, which can be halved again after it's been toasted.

CORIANDER CHUTNEY DIP

1/2 cup of fresh cilantro, chopped fine
2 large Tablespoons green chile chutney
2 large Tablespoons mayonnaise

Mix all ingredients and serve with naan, quartered and lightly toasted.

Italian Markets

Cosolo's Italian Market

8000 E. Quincy 290-8950
Monday–Friday, 10 am–6 pm; Saturday, 9 am–6 pm.
Closed Sunday.

It's not often that you walk into a market and the first thing the owner draws your attention to is the antacid. However, that's what happens when I first walk into Cosolo's and meet Jean Kopecky, who runs this lovely Italian deli with her partner, Shirley Kadell. The antacid is called brioschi and it fizzes in your mouth. Lots of people really like it, according to Jean.

This doesn't mean that the food here doesn't please the palate. You can find fresh pasta, laid out in the deli case where you can see it instead of packaged up and hidden in the refrigerator case, hand-rolled ravioli, pasta sauces and pesto, and one of their most popular items: a pizza kit. This includes dough, sauce, cheeses, and makes an 18" pizza. It's especially popular on Friday nights–when nobody wants to cook!

The Italian meats and cheeses are all fresh and delicious–salami, cappocollo, Parma ham, Asiago, Parmesan, Bel Paese, Gorgonzola and Romano to name a few. Oh–and don't forget mozzarella and marscapone. They also have fresh, homemade sausage, olives and take-and-bake lasagne.

Almost everything here is either imported or homemade. Packaged polenta, olive oils, vinegars, whole chestnuts, bread sticks, panettone–if it's Italian, they've got it. They even have pasta machines, for those of us who are energetic and skilled enough to make our own pasta. Twelve different salad dressings, and for dessert, how about some cheesecake? Or a party tray of biscotti and other mixed cookies, just to round out a great Italian meal.

Mancinelli's Italian Market

3245 Osage 433-9449
Tuesday–Friday, 8 am–5:30 pm; Saturday, 8 am–5 pm.
Closed Sunday & Monday.

Mancinelli's Market has been in business seventy one years. Now run by Tony Senior and Tony Junior, it was started by Tony Junior's grandfather, back when the neighborhood was all Italian. Mancinelli's is famous for homemade pasta, like ravioli and tortellini, and rightly so. They also make their own sweet cannoli filling with ricotta cheese, and their own spaghetti sauce.

You can buy semolina and durum flour here. Both are used in various combinations to make different kinds of fresh pasta. I particularly like their capocollo, their Italian spices, like basil, oregano, rosemary and bay leaves, sold in bulk and remarkably inexpensive compared to those little bottles you buy in the supermarket, and

their Italian cheeses, like Romano, Asiago and Parmesan. Olive oils, vinegars and sweet peppers are available, and so is fresh bread. Their bulk olives are always good, and I notice that there are dried chestnuts, ready to be reconstituted for wonderful holiday stuffings!

Father and son make their own Italian sausage, both hot and sweet. They also have a limited selection of fresh meats, which are of high quality. You can always count on a smile and a welcome at Mancinelli's. It's probably the oldest Italian market in town. I like it.

Vinnola's Market

7750 W. 38th Avenue, Wheat Ridge 421-3955
Monday–Friday, 9 am–6 pm; Saturday, 9 am–5:30 pm.
Closed Sunday.

Vinnola's is a medium-sized Italian market with Italian cheeses and sausage, like fontina, Asiago and mozzarella, and prosciutto, salami, mortadella and several kinds of dry sausage. A large selection of Italian olive oils, vinegars, bottled peppers, giardiniera (Italian pickled antipasto salad vegetables) and a selection of canned fava, lupini and cannellini beans, are prominently displayed.

If you're looking for Italian flavorings for cakes or cookies, they have the most extensive

collection I've ever seen. Although they're not labeled in English, someone behind the counter can usually explain what flavor they are.

Pastas, both dried and fresh, are many and various. Vinnola's is also a bakery, with very tasty Italian bread and other baked goods, including sweet cannolis, éclairs and cream puffs. Their garlic toast makes perfect croutons.

There's quite a large seating area, and Vinnola's does a healthy lunch business.

Kosher Markets

Steinberg's Kosher Grocery

4017 W. Colfax 534-0314
Tuesday–Thursday, 9 am–6 pm; Friday, 9 am–3:30 pm;
Sunday, 10 am–5 pm. Closed Saturday & Monday.

This is an all-kosher grocery store in the old Jewish neighborhood on the West side of town. They carry kosher meats, chicken, smoked salmon spread, Danish Brie, lox, feta cheese and many other kosher delicacies. I wasn't surprised to find fresh challah (egg bread) rolls, borscht, matzoh or egg noodles, and was happy to find hummus, in tins and mixes, as well as lots of great fish like caviar, gefilte fish and sardines.

This is part of what was once a large number of kosher shops and delis in this neighborhood. Yiddish is still spoken here routinely. This is a store where time seems to have stood still. It's an experience.

Utica Grocery

4500 W. Colfax 534-2253
Monday–Thursday, around 9:30 am–6 pm; Friday, 9:30 am–2 pm.
Closed Saturday. Sunday, 10 am–5 pm.

On the corner of Colfax and Utica is a little kosher market, one of a few shops left from the old Jewish neighborhood that thrived on the West side. Of course, there's still a Jewish neighborhood here, served by the three or four remaining shops. But there used to be an entire row of kosher shops–a grocery, bakery, meat market, fish market. The Utica Grocery has been in this spot for over 40 years. Now it's owned by Bruce Goldner. He's out of town when I visit, but the store is being run by a friend of his, who's friendly and has lived in the neighborhood all her life–so she remembers all the old stores–a whole row of them all the way down to the viaduct–and the boys' school down the block.

This is the place to go if you have a yen for gefilte fish, whitefish, matzoh or Jewish egg bread. They have ten different brands of sardines, fish and kosher meats, which are healthy and free range without chemicals for the most part. Stepping into this grocery store is like stepping into another time, when people did all their shopping at the neighborhood groceries instead of at the supermarkets.

JEWISH INGREDIENTS

Bagel: *A ring-shaped bread roll, first boiled, then baked in the oven*

Blintz: *A thin pancake stuffed with various fillings, often ricotta cheese, and topped with sour cream*

Borscht: *Beet or cabbage soup, served hot or cold. Sometimes contains meat. Often served cold with a dollop of sour cream–though not if the soup contains meat and the kitchen is kosher!*

Challah: *Egg bread, often braided into fancy shapes for Sabbath or holidays*

Farfel: *Small pieces of broken noodles, often used in soup*

Gefilte fish: *Mixture of ground fish, matzoh meal, eggs and vegetables shaped into balls and poached. Traditionally served with horseradish*

Kasha: *Buckwheat groats, a grain served as a side dish for meat, often mixed with noodles*

Kishke: *Beef casing, filled with seasonal stuffing and roasted. Also known as derma*

Knishes: *Stuffed dumplings, usually filled with potatoes or meat*

Kugel: *Potatoes or noodles combined with eggs and baked in the oven like a pudding. Can be served as a side dish or sweetened and served as a dessert*

Mandelbrot: *Crisp, twice-baked almond cookies*

Matzoh: *Unleavened bread traditionally served during the eight days of Passover*

Schmaltz: *Rendered chicken fat, often used instead of butter or margarine*

Tzimmes: *A mixture of sweet potatoes, carrots, and dried fruit, made into a pudding*

Varnishkes: *Noodle dough shaped like bow-ties, traditionally served with kasha*

Mexican &
South American Markets

846 Santa Fe Drive 534-7020
Friday & Saturday, 10 am – 6 pm.

A really complete line of Southwestern food items is available at this wonderful market. They always have something delicious simmering on the burner to lure you in off Santa Fe Drive for a spicy taste treat of hominy and bean stew or green chile. It's really fun to visit and try all the great things they cook up here. They have recently only been open Fridays and Saturdays because Charles has been concentrating on selling his Big Chili line wholesale instead of retail. However, they still have a great diversity of dried chilis (Charles drives down to New Mexico, starting in late July, and brings the chilis back and roasts them himself all through the summer until the first frost ends the New Mexico chile season sometime in mid-October.)

There's a very complete selection of Mexican and Southwestern spices, including some that are quite hard to find, like Mormon tea. They also have dried beans, lots of salsas and wonderful gift items like red and green chile jelly and Sante Fe mustard. The Big Chili line has lots of spice mixes that make it easy to whip up professional-tasting Mexican and Southwestern dishes. Biscochito mix, pico de gallo mix, habanero salsa mix, frijoles spice mix, sopapilla mix, green chili mix–these are just some of the options.

Their salsas are also quite varied: Santa Fe salsa, Chimayo red chile sauce, and the great Santa Fe Ole sauces: cactus, chipotle, green chile and others. Blue posole and achiote paste are available too.

You can buy frozen green chiles year-round, and several varieties of chile pods are available dried: New Mexico red chiles from the Rio Grande valley, as well as chile pasilla, habanero–the world's hottest chile–, cascabel, and ancho, among others. The atmosphere here is friendly and relaxed, which makes it a great place to browse.

The Chili Store

Valle Grande Products, Inc., 4320-D Morrison Road
936-9309 936-4274
Monday–Saturday, 8 am–5:30 pm. Closed Sunday.

This little store is in a most unusual location, right off Morrison Road and Stuart. You could easily drive by and not notice it since it sits way back off the road. The store is run by Leonora and Clifford McNutt, who own Valle Grande Products. They sell wholesale and retail, and have a great selection of Mexican and Southwestern foodstuffs. Cliff and Leonora are from the Hatch Valley in New Mexico, so they know all about chiles. They have frozen, peeled and roasted green chiles and puréed red chiles and bags of dried chipotles (smoked jalapenos).

As well as sacks of beans, masa mixta for making tamales, the hojas or corn shucks to put the tamales into, chicharrones and tortilla chips, they have tortillas made especially for them and they make their own sopapillas. I've never seen dried green jalapeno powder like they have at The Chili Store, and some of their other mixes are quite unusual–they make their own El Toro style chile mix (does it taste like the hot breath of the bull?) carne adovada mix, fajita mix, and several kinds of ground and crushed chiles. Blue corn atole is available, as well as annatto seed, used in South American cooking, chorizo mix for making your own sausage and chile para menudo. Menudo is Mexican tripe soup.

Peñafiel is a brand of Mexican sodas–difficult to find and absolutely delicious, and you can get it here. They also have a brand called Jarritos, which I'm not familiar with, which comes in green and yellow. Leonora says the yellow is pineapple, which sounds good!

Leonora's daughter and son-in-law are learning about the business, so this is going to stay a family business. It's a pleasure to visit this little store and discover all the hidden treasures they have here.

HANDLING CHILES

Chiles contain oils that can burn your eyes and skin many hours after you've finished handling them. Even washing your hands with soap and water often doesn't get rid of the irritating substance. Wearing rubber gloves is the best way to handle chiles–and wash the gloves and your hands thoroughly afterwards.

BLUE CORN MUSH

5-1/2 cups reserved chicken broth from filling below
2 cups blue cornmeal
Chopped cilantro

Bring 5-1/2 cups reserved chicken broth to boil. Add 2 cups blue cornmeal. Stir till smooth. Cook over low heat 15 minutes. Line casserole with 1/2 cornmeal mush. Put in chicken mole filling (below). Top with the rest of the mush. Bake 1 hour at 350°. Top with chopped cilantro and serve.

BLUE CORN TAMALE PIE WITH CHICKEN MOLE FILLING

Filling
1 chicken (2–3 lbs.)
1 large onion, chopped
5 large carrots, chopped
3–4 cloves garlic
1 bay leaf
Water to cover
Mole sauce

Cook chicken, vegetables and spices in water to cover for 3/4 hour. Drain and reserve liquid. Skin and debone chicken, chopping with carrots and onions. Stir in mole sauce (from specialty grocery or gourmet section of supermarket) to taste. Add to corn mush above.

El Azteca Grocery

1065 Federal Blvd 893-3642
Daily, 8 am–6 pm. Closed Sunday.

I came across El Azteca quite by accident, as I was driving south on Federal in search of all the little Asian markets there. Seeing the sign, I screeched to a halt–and was really glad I did! This little market, which makes burritos to take out and offers a small but interesting variety of Argentinian specialties, is run by Lucia, a former nurse, who believes it's her task to help out the entire world! What a pleasure she is to talk to–and she has some really wonderful South American foods.

Yerba maté tea is available at El Azteca, and Lucia asserts that many people, not only from South America, but from all over, come here to buy it. She shows me a little gourd that they use in Argentina to drink the maté from, and a small silver spoon-like device with a strainer on the end, called a bombilla, that the maté goes into to steep.

She also sells dulce de leche (cream of caramel) in jars, figs and pumpkins in syrup, a sweet potato dessert from Argentina, and an Argentinian quince jam. She has a few Mexican-style pastries, and small containers of flan in the refrigerator case.

There are some of the more usual Hispanic products here–dried chiles, large bags of dried beans, masa mixta for making tortillas, chorizo and a rack of spices, many of which are for tea, like manzanilla (chamomile), orange flowers and jasmine. While I was there, someone called looking for medicinal herbs, and Lucia told me the story of a man who'd had hiccups for two years almost continuously, who was

cured when he tried the right herb from her collection.

I tried some of her non-alcoholic aperitif from Argentina and it is superb! Made with herbs and sucrose, it's called Terma and it's absolutely delicious. It has the depth and substance of a liqueur, but with an intriguing herbal edge. The closest thing to it would be vermouth. A real find–just like El Azteca.

Johnny's Grocery & Market

2030 Larimer 297-0155
Monday–Saturday, 9 am–6 pm. Closed Sunday.

Helen and Eddie Maestas run this neighborhood market with great energy and goodwill. They have homemade chorizo and carne adovada (spicy marinated pork), as well as homemade green chile, menudo and chicharrones (pork rinds), chiles rellenos, and, in the summer, carnitas barbocoa (barbecued beef, which I tasted–it was spicy and tender, melting in my mouth with flavor–delicious). They make different kinds of burritos every day, and also have steak and chicken ready to take out.

The meat market in the back is surprising, and Eddie told me they have things I'm probably not very familiar with: pigs' ears, pigs' tails, pigs' snouts, lamb and hog head meat, brains, tongues, and beef intestines. He's right. Helen loves to cook, so I know she can supply some great recipes for these cuts of meat. In the front of the store are many different kinds of chile, both crushed and ground, and some mixes I hadn't seen in other places: spice for menudo, salsa mix, chorizo mix and prepared masa, as well as the corn husks to put it into to make tamales. They have a nice selection of Mexican dried spices, with perhaps more varieties of dried chile than usual: chile de arbol, chile ancho, chile mulato, chile caribe and chile pasilla. There is also a fresh vegetable section with tomatillos, fresh jalapenos and other fresh vegetables.

All the other necessities for Mexican-style cooking are available too, including beans, posole, lard, and garlic.

In season, Johnny's has New Mexico chile ristras and at Christmas they have a great selection of pinatas. I bought some jamaica tea–hibiscus, which has to be boiled in hot water but turns a lovely rose color and has a delicate flowery taste. It's really good with sweetener as hot tea or iced.

Helen and Eddie have run Johnny's Market for the last 17 years. Eddie worked in the neighborhood for 10 years before that, at Western Beef. Johnny's has tasty prepared meats, unusual mixes for Mexican dishes and a fine selection of chiles.

CHILES

There are over 7,000 varieties of chiles or chilis growing throughout the world. They are totally unrelated to true pepper (piper nigrum) and belong to the genus capsicum, which belongs to the same family as tomatoes, potatoes and eggplant. When the Spanish explorers first tasted chiles in the Caribbean, they thought they were like the black pepper they knew and named them peppers. The most common chiles found in our markets in Colorado are:

Chile Ancho: *Ripened, dried chile poblano, can be mild to very spicy*

Anaheim Chile: *Large, bright green peppers with firm, thick flesh and relatively mild flavor*

Chile Arbol: *Small, dried, brick orange, very spicy chile*

Chile Caribe: *Grown in northern New Mexico, a little larger than the pequin (above). Hot with a sweet, spicy flavor*

Chile Cascabel: *Small, round chile, sounds like a rattle if you shake it. Pleasant nutty flavor*

Chile Chipotle: *Dried, smoked jalapeño chile, with characteristic smoky flavor, usually sold canned in adobo sauce. Lala's Mexican Deli smokes their own—and they're sweeter than the canned variety.*

Chile Jalapeño: *Small, round, dark green and red. Hot to very hot*

New Mexico Green Chile: *Similar to Anaheim peppers, but hotter. Also found in a dried, red (ripened) form*

Chile Pasilla: *Brownish-black dried chile, rich tasting and spicy*

Chile Pequin: *Very tiny, wild chiles. Extremely hot*

Chile Poblano: *Large, dark green, looks similar to a bell pepper. Usually has a mild, full flavor, but can sometimes be quite hot. When ripened and dried, it becomes known as chile ancho.*

Chile Serrano: *Small, light green chili, sometimes very thin. Very hot*

Thai Chiles: *These small dried red chiles are extremely hot.*

CHICKEN WITH TOMATILLO SAUCE

1/2 onion, chopped
4 carrots, chopped
2 cloves elephant garlic, chopped
4 cloves garlic, minced
2 teaspoon New Mexico red pepper
2 tablespoons cooking oil
One 3 lb. chicken
6 chicken thighs
2 cans chicken broth
2 cans Mexican chile verde sauce with tomatillos (Herdes brand)
1/4 bunch fresh cilantro
3 tablespoons cumin
3 tablespoons flour

Saute onion, carrots, elephant garlic and garlic in the cooking oil over medium heat for 5–8 minutes or until soft but not browned. Add red pepper and chicken and chicken thighs. Cover with chicken broth and one can of water. Cook until the chicken falls from the bone easily—about 45 minutes. Take out the chicken and debone. Remove skin and break chicken into bite-sized pieces.

Add cumin to sauce and mix. Put sauce into blender and puree. Put flour into bottom of a large, clean saucepan or casserole. Add pureed sauce gradually, until flour and cumin is dissolved. Put chicken pieces back into the sauce and heat gently. Serve or refrigerate and serve later. Serves 6–8.

PINON TART
(Barbara Wright)

1–9" tart shell
4 tablespoons butter
3/4 cup brown sugar
1 tablespoon egg white
1/4 teaspoon vanilla
1/2 teaspoon cognac
2 cups piñon nuts

Cream butter, beat in sugar, then rest of ingredients. Add nuts, spread into shell with fingers. Bake in 400° oven for 15 minutes.

La Popular Tortillas & Tamales

2012 Larimer 296-1687
Daily, 9 am–6 pm; Sunday, 9 am–4 pm.

This family-owned business is reputed to have the best tamales in town. They also make their own fresh tortillas and on Tuesday and Thursday they have fresh, homemade masa–the corn dough used to make tamales and corn tortillas. It's made from dried white corn kernels cooked with lime in copious amounts of water. They also have the corn husks to put the tamales into, but most people prefer to just buy their homemade tamales.

La Popular also has Mexican bread, and a selection of pastries like empanadas with vanilla cream, strawberry, pineapple or apple filling, pumpkin empanadas in cinnamon dough and cookies, including peanut butter cookies and short-bread cookies with raspberry jam. Their selection of Mexican spices is better than the average, with their own brand of green chile powder as well as packets of chile caribe, pasilla, and chile ancho pods. They also sell atole, the corn meal mixture used in soup.

La Popular is a very friendly place to shop. I spoke to Michael, son of Jesse Delatorre. Jesse and his brother Elias own the store. Their tortillas and tamales are terrific!

Middle Eastern & Greek Markets

Arash Supermarket

2159 S. Parker Road 752-9272
Monday–Saturday, 10 am–9 pm; Sunday, 10 am–6 pm.

A Persian market? Yes, indeed! Mehran Diva, the owner, is an Iranian from Azerdbijan, and his market offers a range of Persian and Turkish foods, including basmati rice, chicory essence for coffee, olives and an entire shelf of different teas. They have a very extensive rack of spices, and a collection of interesting preserves: fig jam, apricot and sour cherry preserves, as well as a lot of tahini and olive oil.

There are several different kinds of olives and Bulgarian and French feta cheese. A yoghurt drink which is very Persian, according to Mehran, is called doogh, but we can't find one with that name on it. They're simply called yoghurt drink or carbonated yoghurt drink.

There are teapots and coffee warmers and a good selection of pickles and chutneys. Also, they have several kinds of bread, including lavosh, which I buy to try. Surprisingly, there is a good Italian mortadella (smoked sausage heavily seasoned with garlic) and not so surprisingly, several kinds of halvah. My favorite find here is small tins of heavy whipped cream, just like I used to buy in England. It's very thick and tasty, almost like Devon cream, and perfect on scones, over fresh berries or with pie instead of icecream!

MIDDLE EASTERN/GREEK FOOD GUIDE

Baklava: *A dessert made with layers of phyllo dough, nuts and honey*

Basterma: *Dried beef coated with spices, sliced thinly and used for sandwiches*

Bulgur: *Dried wheat used in tabouli salad or as a substitute for rice*

Couscous: *Grain made from the heart of durum wheat, finely ground, parboiled and dried*

Dolma, dolmades: *Leaves stuffed with meat, rice or other filling*

Falafel: *Seasoned, fried garbanzo bean cakes or balls*

Feta: *Semi-soft white cheese made from goat's or sheep's milk*

Hummus: *Garbanzo bean dip, often made with tahini (sesame seed butter) as hummus-bi-tahini*

Halva, halvah: *A sweet made with flour of various kinds or carrots*

Harissa: *Hot sauce for North African and Middle Eastern cooking*

Kasseri: *Firm cheese made from goat or sheep's milk*

Kefalotiri: *Hard cheese used for grating, equivalent to Parmesan or Romano*

Lavash: *Round or oval cracker bread*

Pita: *Arab or Greek pocket bread*

Sumac: *Seasoning used in North African and Greek cooking*

Syrian cheese: *Resembles Monterey Jack or Muenster cheese*

Tahini: *A sesame seed paste or butter*

Tarama: *Roe of carp used to make dips (can be red or white)*

Taramosalata: *Dip made from tarama or carp roe*

Zatar: *Blend of spices including thyme, marjoram and sumac*

Economy Greek Market

1035 Lincoln 861-3001
Monday–Friday, 7 am–5:30 pm; Saturday, 9 am–5 pm.
Closed Sunday.

This market is named not after the inexpensiveness of its products, but after its first owner, Mr. Economy, (probably Mr. Ekonoumos whose name was changed at Ellis Island) who started this Greek super-market on Market Street in 1901. At that time the store had a Greek bakery as well, making Greek bread, pullman loaves (oblong-shaped loaves of bread made especially to be cut for sandwiches) and pies. Mr. Economy used to supply mining towns like Erie, Frederick and Brighton with baked goods and groceries, taking them out there personally to feed the Greeks, Bulgarians, Romanians, and Italians who worked in the mines.

This story is told by Mr. Economy's son, also Mr. Economy, who now works in the store, although he doesn't own it anymore. The deli case contains several kinds of cheese, including feta, kasseri (sheep's milk cheese, hard and sharp in flavor), kefalotire and Syrian cheese. There are meats like basturma, a kind of dried spiced beef, and many kinds of olives. There are also sweet, honey-flavored desserts like baklava and khourambes and kataifi. Pignolia (pine nuts) are also kept, correctly, in the refrigerated deli case so they don't get rancid-tasting. Behind the counter are bulk spices, some of which are familiar –whole cardamom, dill, cumin, fenugreek, and some which aren't–like zatar, a combination of spices used in Middle Eastern cooking, according to Mr. Economy. I later look it up, and find it's a Greek herb mix-ture that's a blend of thyme and oregano. They also have sumac, which I've used in Middle Eastern dishes. It's great–it gives a nice tang, depth of flavor and pungency to tagines and stews.

Greek taramosalata, pepper-oncini peppers, stuffed grape leaves (in jars or in enormous cans for party size!) make me start thinking of Greek salads with pita bread (which they also have here, of course). There are several kinds of halvah, both fla-vored and plain, tahini (sesame seed butter used in making hummus), and large cans of olive oil. Also available is dried apricot paste, dried fava beans, red lentils, basmati rice, green broad beans in cans, and three kinds of bulghur wheat: fine, medium or coarse.

GREEK FISH WITH BREAD AND GARLIC SAUCE

2 large onions, sliced
2 lbs. fresh white fish fillets, like sole, flounder or perch
1 can (15 oz.) tomatoes
1/4 cup olive oil
1/3 cup chopped parsley
2 sliced lemons
1 slice bread
2–3 garlic cloves, minced
1/3 cup olive oil
1/3 cup vinegar
1/2 teaspoon salt, if needed

Grease shallow baking pan. Arrange sliced onions in the bottom. Put fish on top of onions. Chop tomatoes a little. Add them with the first 1/4 cup olive oil and parsley and pour over fish. Place lemon slices on top. Bake uncovered for 30–45 minutes at 400° or until fish is flaky.

Meanwhile, dip bread in hot water and squeeze dry. Mash with remaining ingredients, including vinegar and olive oil. Add salt if needed. Place fish, with tomatoes and onions, on serving dish. Serve with bread sauce. Dinner for 4.

LAMOONADA

5 large lemons
7 cups water
Sugar or sweetener to taste
Orange flower water
Ice cubes
6 mint sprigs

Squeeze lemon juice into a jug. Set aside. Heat water and pour over mint sprigs and lemon shells. Melt sugar in hot water. Let steep for 1–2 hours. Add lemon juice, squeeze out lemon shells and strain. Add orange flower water–about 10 drops. Serve over ice cubes garnished with a slice of lemon peel and a mint sprig. Serves 6.

International Market

2020 S. Parker Road 695-1090
Daily, 10 am – 9 pm.

The International Market is a real find, with food from the Middle East, India and Africa. The selection of dried yellow and green peas, fava beans and many kinds of dal–Indian lentils, beans and peas–is spectacular. So is the array of different grains and flour–bulghur, farina, corn flour, rice flour, semolina and roasted gram flour, to name a few. Gram flour is made from Bengal peas, a kind of chickpea or garbanzo. The Indian chutneys include such favorites as

mango and coriander, and there are syrups and pickles as well.

There is a good selection of Middle Eastern, Indian and other breads–from chapati and pita to lavosh and tortillas. (Lavosh is a large, oval, flat bread). There are many kinds of noodles, ground cassava and cassava flour, Nigerian red pepper, Indian ghee, tahini and felafel mix, and olive oils from

Lebanon, Spain and Tunisia. Nuts are refrigerated to keep them from becoming rancid: cashews, hazelnuts, slivered almonds. Also in the refrigerator case is phyllo dough for making baklava, and other great flaky pastries, and kataifi, a kind of shredded wheat-type dough that makes great desserts. They cut and package their own meat, and they have lamb shank, oxtail, goat liver, lamb shoulder and leg and lamb chops. There are many kinds of olives, and several Middle

Eastern cheeses. Greek tarama (carp roe) for taramosalata is also available. Taramosalata is a dip made with carp roe, bread, olive oil and lemon juice.

The dessert case is a wonder of small, bite-sized baked goods. A party tray with a selection for $19.95 would feed a large dinner party. I've tried some, and they were flavored with rosewater, delicate and delicious! The International Market has food from almost anywhere under the sun. They really live up to their name.

AFRICAN CHICKEN PEANUT STEW

6 cups good quality homemade chicken broth
1 small can (6 oz.) tomato paste
1 cup smooth peanut butter
1 teaspoon cayenne hot sauce, or to taste
2 cups diced chicken meat
2 cups diced, sautéed green, red and yellow peppers

Add broth to tomato paste, peanut butter and hot sauce in a pan. Heat. Add chicken and peppers. Skim off oil. Season to taste.

CHICKEN BREASTS WITH ORANGE FLOWER WATER

4 chicken breasts, washed and skinned
2 cloves garlic, peeled
6 pieces crystallized ginger
4 teaspoons orange flower water
Juice of 1 lemon
3 tablespoons honey
3 tablespoons olive oil

Crush garlic and whirl with all other ingredients except chicken breasts in food processor or blender. Marinate chicken in this mixture in the refrigerator overnight if possible, or at least 4 hours. Broil chicken breasts and serve with couscous. Serves 4.

COUSCOUS

It's delicious and authentic cooked in the following manner:
In microwave or in small saucepan, heat 2 cups chicken broth. When it boils, add 1 cup couscous. Cover and let sit 10-15 minutes. Then turn out onto a large plate. Add 1 tablespoon olive oil and rub between your fingers until all the grains are coated. Put couscous into a bowl and reheat in microwave at serving time.

TABOULI SALAD

1 cup fine bulghur wheat, washed
1-1/2 cups finely chopped parsley
1/2 cup finely chopped red onion
1/2 cup finely chopped fresh mint
1/4 cup lemon juice
1/2 teaspoon sumac
1/2 teaspoon black pepper
1/4 cup olive oil
1/2 cup each chopped tomatoes and cucumber
Salt to taste
1 head romaine lettuce

Drain bulghur and squeeze in a clean towel. Mix with onions, mint, lemon juice, sumac and pepper. Toss with oil, tomatoes and cucumber. Taste and add salt if needed. Wash lettuce and separate leaves. Serve the bulghur mixture with leaves around it so that guests can scoop up the bulghur with the leaves and eat. Serves 6.

COUSCOUS TAGINE

1/4 cup olive oil
1 pound stewing lamb, cut in pieces
3–4 lb chicken
1 large onion, chopped
4 carrots, sliced
3 parsnips, cut into chunks
2–4 cloves garlic, depending on size
2 teaspoons cinnamon
1 teaspoon ground cloves
1/2 teaspoon ground black pepper
1 cup tomato sauce
1–3 tablespoons harissa
1-1/2 tablespoons cumin
1 tablespoon sumac
2 lemon omani (preserved lemons)
2 cups each, beef and chicken broth
2 potatoes, washed, unpeeled and cut into chunks
3 large parsnips, peeled and cut into chunks
Salt to taste

Heat olive oil in large casserole. Sauté onions and carrots slowly in oil over medium heat for about 10 minutes. Add lamb pieces and brown, pushing vegetables to the side. Add spices, crushed garlic, tomato sauce and harissa. Add parsnips. Put lamb and chicken into pot and add beef and chicken broth to cover, and a little water if necessary. Cook slowly 1 hour. Add potatoes. Taste and correct seasoning. Cook 1 hour longer or until tender. Serve over couscous.

GARBANZO BEAN DIP

1 can garbanzo beans, drained
6 Tablespoons tahini (sesame seed paste)
2 large cloves garlic, pressed
2 teaspoons 7-spice mixture (Middle East Market)
1-1/2 teaspoons sumac
2 teaspoons cumin
2 teaspoons–2 tablespoons olive oil (enough to make a mayonnaise-like consistency)

Whirl garbanzos with tahini and olive oil in food processor or blender or mash with a fork. Add spices. Serve with pita triangles or naan or slices of crusty French bread.

TUNISIAN CHICKEN WITH OLIVES AND GARLIC

4 tablespoons olive oil
6 lbs. chicken, cut into pieces
1/2 cup minced onion
10 garlic cloves, minced
4 bay leaves
1 teaspoon salt, or to taste
1 teaspoon pepper
2 cups dry red wine
1/2 cup tomato paste
4 teaspoons chipotles in adobo, mashed (or to taste)
4 cups chicken broth
1 cup good quality green olives, pitted

Heat oil in heavy skillet on medium high heat. Wash chicken pieces and pat dry. Brown in skillet. Add onion, garlic, bay leaves, salt and pepper. Cook 5 minutes. Pour in wine and reduce sauce. Blend in tomato paste. Reduce heat to low. Add chicken broth. Cover and cook 20 minutes. Add olives and cook till chicken is done, about 5 minutes. Serves 4–6.

Middle East Market

2254 S. Colorado Boulevard 756-4580
Daily, 10 am – 9 pm (approximately)

Middle East Market is a delightful, well-stocked market hidden away in a strip shopping center just north of Evans on Colorado Boulevard.

The owner, Yousef Madhun, is very knowledgeable about food from all over the Middle East, and he has an enormous variety of goods. In his deli case you'll find fifteen varieties of olives, from Greek kalamata and kolossa to Moroccan oil-cured. He has five different kinds of feta, including double cream, as well as Syrian cheese, several kinds of halvah and Turkish delight.

Desserts are made of phyllo or kataifi and honey. They include burma, which is very rich, ghribah, baklava with pistachios or walnuts, and other wonderful sweet treats. In his refrigerator case are many kinds of ethnic bread, including pita, whole wheat and white, Indian naan, Afghani taftoon (an onion flat bread), to name just a few. He carries pine nuts, slivered almonds, dried apricots and big bags of dates, which they eat as a snack with tea in Middle Eastern countries. He also has dried currants, golden prunes, barberries and sour cherries.

His sodas are quite exotic, such as as mango and guava juices and a yoghurt soda (mint and plain versions) that I hadn't seen anywhere else until I dis-covered the Persian market! Yousef claims to have over 30 different varieties of tea (I don't doubt it for a minute) and coffee from Ethiopia and Tanzania, Saudi and Turkish roasts and even green, unroasted coffee beans.

His collection of olive oils is extensive, and so is the choice of herbs and spices sold by the ounce. You can find cardamom, fenugreek, basil, poppy seeds, sumac and many others. I use the 7-spice mixture in my couscous, but I really don't know exactly what's in it. There is a good selection of Indian chutneys, pickles and curry mixes. Beans, both dried and canned, come in many varieties, such as fava, red beans, lentils, garbanzos and split peas.

This is one of the most inexpensive places I've found to buy orange flower water, rose water, and mint water. These waters add a delicate flavor to desserts and other Middle Eastern dishes. Frozen phyllo and kataifi are both dough for making pastries, and you can find them here.

Middle Eastern food is complex and subtly flavored. Here's where you can find all the ingredients for your Middle East feast, except the belly dancer!

Russian Markets

5225 Leetsdale 321-7144
Tuesday–Saturday, 9 am–7 pm; Sunday, 10 am–6 pm.
Closed Monday.

So why does the European Mart have an advertisement for New York pastries and cakes in the window? I only wonder this for a moment. As soon as I walk into this attractive little deli on Leetsdale and Forest and see the delectable cakes and pastries in the case, I know why. Yummm! The pastries are quite beautiful, and taste just as good as they look. Owners Dmitry Gershengorin and his sister Eugenia have put together an impressive collection of Eastern European comestibles during the three years they've been in business here and many of their customers are Russians and Poles who've found a little taste of home and keep coming back for more.

The deli case contains smoked fish, herring, salami and cold cuts, and cheeses imported from Denmark and Finland, among other places. Neuchatel cheese from Switzerland and chocolate butter spread made with kefir are also available.

The fabled New York pastries are delivered twice weekly and include napoleons, almond pastries and something Dmitry describes as a margarita. Cookies include wafer rolls made with halvah cream and several kinds of butter cookies. Jars of pickled cabbage, pickled onions, sauerkraut, olives, and Hungarian pickles line the shelves, while in bins on the floor are kasha, whole groats and dried beans available in bulk.

Unusual juices include carrot juice from Switzerland, blackcurrant, apple, strawberry, and sour cherry juice in boxes. There are also teas and tisanes like rosehip and hibiscus, melange de tisanes fruitées (tisane made with mixed fruits) and my personal favorite, lindenflower tea.

There is a selection of Russian newspapers and some gift items, like Russian dolls and painted eggs. Spices in bulk are also available.

Specialty Markets, Gourmet & Gift Shops

Alfalfa's

Cherry Creek, 3rd & University 320-0700
Monday–Saturday, 8 am–10 pm; Sunday, 8 am–9 pm.
Capitol Hill, 11th & Ogden 832-7701
Monday–Saturday, 7:30 am–9:30 pm; Sunday, 8 am–9 pm.
Littleton, Orchard & University 798-9699
Daily, 8 am–9 pm.

All the Alfalfa's stores are beautiful, with organic produce, a coffee and juice bar and an astonishing array of cheeses. I found Brie, goat cheeses, Sage Derby from England, Stilton, Double Gloucester, and raw milk cheeses. Their produce usually includes a large number of fresh exotic mushrooms in season, like morels, shiitake and cremini, gourmet greens including my favorite, arugula, red, yellow and often orange and purple bell peppers, organic tomatoes, tomatillos, and many, many other usual and unusual vegetables, all of above average quality.

They have a wonderful bakery with breads, muffins and scones as well as some of the most mouth-watering tortes I've seen. Roger's Bread is a dessert

bread that's simply delicious, and I've never found it anywhere else. Try it! They also have chocolates in some stores.

There's an assortment of balsamic vinegars and olive oils, as well as wonderful salsas, chutneys, sauces and lots of imported pastas and grains. Wild rice, pearl barley, amaranth, blue organic cornmeal, beans and flours are available here. Olive and safflower oil, maple syrup and tamari are available in bulk, as are pastas and grains. They sell herbs, fresh and dried, and fresh pasta and chile sauces. Dried herbs and teas can be bought in bulk.

Their teas and coffees are varied, as are their crackers, chips and cookies. These stores combine gourmet and natural foods and they're a pleasure to visit. You're sure to find some special thing that catches your eye and pretty soon you can't do without it. This happened to me with torta, a mixture of cream cheese and Parmesan, dried tomatoes and pesto. It's just one of those fabulous discoveries that makes life more exciting. If you visit Alfalfa's, you're bound to find something you can't live without.

Aromas Market

2510 S. Colorado Boulevard 759-0889
Monday–Friday, 11 am–7 pm; Saturday, 10 am–6 pm.
Sunday, noon–5 pm.

This beautifully appointed market has all kinds of gourmet deli and grocery items, like gourmet pastas, many different kinds of olive oils and balsamic vinegars, salad dressings and coffees, teas and Italian sodas. Their coffee by the pound is heavy on blends served in Denver's past and present restaurants: Dudley's, Cliff Young's, Tante Louise. They also have decaf. and flavored coffees.

You can get a caffe latte or a cappuccino here and wander around and look at the other goodies they have on the shelves. On the sweet side, they have lots of jellies, fruit syrups, chocolates and English toffee, as well as things like instant white chocolate drink mix.

The owners feel that one of their best items is a roasted chicken (choose from lemon pepper, garlic pepper, orange pepper, cajun or Jamaican jerk). You have to order it before 2 p.m. and it will be ready by 4:30 pm. However, I met a woman as I was leaving who was coming there for the gazpacho. "They have the best gazpacho in town," she said. The people who run this place don't qualify as the world's friendliest, in my opinion, but the market is lovely.

Denver Buffalo Company

1109 Lincoln 832-0880
Monday–Friday, 7 am–6 pm; Saturday, 10 am–6 pm. Closed Sunday.

The Denver Buffalo Company restaurant has a good and unusual deli section that adds a cowboy charm to the whole place. The deli case has many varieties of buffalo sausage, including frankfurters, Italian, Polish and bratwurst. There are also other deli meats, like smoked turkey and turkey ham.

The walls are lined with shelves of salsas and other kinds of Western and Southwestern delicacies usually considered gift items, but all excellent quality and equally suitable for home consumption. Chokecherry jelly must be the most flavorful jelly ever conceived in the heart of a pioneer cook, and there are other jellies that look almost as luscious – spruce needle and gooseberry, but then I come across one I've not encountered before–country music jelly? I'd like to hear from someone who's ever tasted any of that! (Please send in your comments–preferably in song!) Microwave corn on the cob is a real novelty, and has that ring of authenticity as well. (Not!)

However, the early pioneers did eat popped corn with milk as a breakfast cereal. I wonder when that went out of style? Red and green chile jelly is one of those great easy but elegant appetizer ideas for serving on top of cream cheese, or mixed with it, surrounded by chips or crackers. Many mustards are available here–of course, it's hardly surprising, since they are probably all great additions to buffalo sausage.

The most unusual product I saw was Tom and Sally's chocolate body paint. This seemed to belong more at Le Bakery Sensual than the Denver Buffalo Company, but perhaps it was a ritual learned from the Native Americans and adapted to the Anglo taste for chocolate. Watkins spices are featured on their own special rack, and there are five different kinds of Watkins pepper: cracked black, cajun, lemon, Mexican and royal.

Friends from the East coast will love this place. It's a taste of the West.

Garramone's Farm Market

10351 W. 44th, Wheat Ridge 422-1346
Daily, 9 am–6 pm. Closed January, February & the first half of March.

Garramone's Farm Market opens with the first signs of spring, and offers a full line of local produce in season. Try their vine-ripened tomatoes, fresh herbs, endive, or their many Western slope items: Palisade cherries, apricots, peaches, corn and tomatoes, by the pound and by the bushel as they come into season.

In the fall, they roast peppers and have pumpkins and other fall items, sell a lot of Christmas trees and then close for the winter.

Their Colorado ristras are less expensive than most, and they have some local jams, honeys and juices that are well worth seeking out. Chokecherry syrup is one of my favorite tastes in the entire world–and you can find it here! Garramone's also carries Merlino's juices: apple, boysenberry, blueberry, and blackberry, among others. In spring and summer you can buy all kinds of bedding plants. This is a family business, lovingly run by Kate and Rick Garramone. The produce is fresh and local and the service is friendly. The store itself is large and airy and gives the impression of a farmer's market. Try them for fresh produce and other local specialty items.

Goosebumps

235 Fillmore 333-0990
Monday–Saturday, 10 am–6 pm; Sunday, noon–5 pm.

This pretty and decorative gift store is one of those nifty, gifty, not for the thrifty Cherry Creek stores. It has cards and gift items for adults and children, and a section of specialty foods, with items from the East coast, like Virginia chopped clams, smoked trout chowder, and, for those who crave them, bottled egg creams. They also have white or dark chocolate popcorn truffles and some fun gift or party items, such as Jewish fortune cookies, wedding fortune cookies, and "naughty but nice" fortune cookies.Some of Uncle Dougie's specialties are available, like the world's most dangerous barbecue sauce, and his torpedo juice for tomato juice cocktail. What is Uncle Dougie, anyway, a pyromaniac?

Western foods are also represented, with items like Dale's Buffalo Chili. This is a place to shop for friends who appreciate food as gifts!

Greens Market

1312 E. 6th Avenue   778-8117
Monday–Friday, 8 am–8 pm; Saturday, 8 am–7 pm; Sunday, 9 am–6 pm.

Michael Nolting, who owns Greens Market, characterizes the place as "healthy gourmet". "It used to be that healthy and gourmet were at opposite ends of the food spectrum," he says. "Now, more and more, the people who want gourmet food also want healthy food–so the two categories are moving closer and closer together."

Greens is an attractive and upscale market that manages to retain a friendly, down-home kind of atmosphere. It never seems rushed or overcrowded, and there are some great products and specialties available. Organic produce is a specialty here, and it always seems fresh and inviting. There's also a fine line of salad dressings to go with all these great veggies. Their herb section is also good.

Pestos of many hues and a small selection of cheeses can be found in the refrigerator case, as well as some unusual prepared foods. Vegetable korma (a mild Indian or Malaysian curry) sits cheek by jowl with artichoke heart pizza, and there are several other exotic kinds of prepared dinners.

The deli case has an eclectic feel as well, with offerings of spinach couscous with almonds, chicken salad, spanakopita (Greek phyllo dough with cheese and spinach) a black-eyed pea salad and hummus. Greens also has a fine supply of different oils–soy, safflower, sunflower and a nice array of olive oils. There are also unusual items like garlic tamari and plum vinegar.

Greens is a good place to go for healthy and unusual high-quality foods. You'll feel welcome here.

Jim Garramone's Fruits and Vegetables

560 S. Holly   320-5561, 320-5597 (24 hour message)
Monday–Saturday, 8 am–7 pm. Closed Sunday.

This specialty food market caters to the surrounding southeast Denver community. They have a wide variety of produce, with above-average quality fruits and vegetables, together with a number of specialty items like tomatillos, dried chile peppers and several kinds of dried mushrooms, such as shiitake, wood ear, paddy straw, porcini and chanterelles.

There's a nice selection of pesto sauces, gourmet vinegars and flavored pastas. Some of the more unusual flavors are curry, teriyaki and saffron. I find an abundance of sauces, chutneys and pickles: salsas, a dried tomato tapenade that makes my mouth water, marinades like Jamaican jerk, hot and mild chow chow, and a Thai peanut

sauce. Vidalia onion, sauerkraut and pickles and an array of preserves including no-sugar blackberry fruit spread.

The frozen food case offer a selection of pastas like ravioli and stuffed shells. This store has quality merchandise and is run by Jim Garramone and his wife Jan.

The Apple Cart

2525 Youngfield, Golden 237-7860
Monday–Friday, 10 am–6 pm; Saturday 10 am–5 pm.
           &

The Lemon Cheese Company

2525 Youngfield, Golden 237-6678
Monday–Friday, 10 am–5:30 pm; Saturday, 10 am–4 pm.

These two gift shops are in the same building but they're actually different stores.

The Apple Cart

The smell of potpourri is so enticing when you walk through the door, it's delicious! And the store itself is equally pretty and inviting, with china and specialty cooking items. There are many unusual gourmet foods here: special pastas, mustards, mulling spices from England and wonderful jams like apricot orange and brandied cranberry conserve. Tomato chips are a novel and delectable find here.

The Lemon Cheese Company

Crossing the bridge like the Billy Goats Gruff (fortunate-ly no troll was on duty!) I find that The Lemon Cheese Company offers still more food specialties. The woman who runs the store has Welsh ancestry, and started making the lemon cheese after a trip to Wales. She also sells scones to go with the lemon cheese–and jams, chutneys and marmalades, as well as coffees and teas, such as Crabtree and Evelyn mango and raspberry. There are lemon cookies, mustards and a variety of china teapots and tea sets, so your experience here can be tasteful as well as tasty. These two places are like quaint gift shops you might find in England or in the restored downtown areas of tourist meccas.

Old Santa Fe Chili Shop

2485 S. Santa Fe Drive 871-9434
Daily, 10 am–6 pm.

If you've ever visited Jackalope in Santa Fe, you'll agree that the Old Santa Fe Chili Shop is the nearest thing we have to it in Denver. They have all kinds of Southwestern gift items, and among them a great many food items that make great gifts for someone else or just for yourself! From cactus relish and chipotle salsa to pico de gallo, popcorn on the cob and chokecherry syrup, they have a fine selection of Santa Fe style foodstuffs that will tempt anyone who ever aspired to serve a Southwestern meal. Their array of dried chiles is enough to inspire me to immediately begin cooking my own authentic chile, practically on the spot!

The Old Santa Fe Chili Shop is really a fun place to go, even if you're not in need of Rocky Mountain green chili mix or prickly pear cactus topping. They also have some gourmet liqueur-flavored coffees and summer mulling spices. Don't forget to look at all the other Santa Fe things they have, like Christmas ornaments, furniture and furnishings and wonderful outdoor ceramics. This place has lots of atmosphere. If you haven't time for a trip to Santa Fe, this is the next best thing.

COOL QUINOA SALAD

(Jennifer Stock, Alfalfa's)

2 cups quinoa
1 cup corn, fresh cut from the cob or frozen
3/4 cup minced red bell pepper
1/2 cup diced cucumber
1/4 cup minced parsley
1-1/2 tablespoons Tamari soy sauce
1 tablespoon rice vinegar
1 tablespoon olive oil

Cook quinoa in 4 cups boiling water until grains pop open and become somewhat translucent. Drain and cool. Stir all ingredients into quinoa and mix well. Cover and refrigerate for at least one hour before serving to allow flavors to marry. Serves 8.

Quinoa is grown primarily in Colorado and South America. It is the highest in protein of any grain. It can be used in salads, soups, casseroles and as a side dish instead of rice or couscous.

The Market

1445 Larimer 534-5140
Monday–Friday, 6:45 am–11 pm; Saturday, 8 am–12 midnight;
Sunday, 8 am–6 pm.

This is a favorite urban hangout on lazy weekend mornings, sitting outside on the sidewalk in Larimer Square if it's warm enough, or snug and warm surrounded by shelves of gourmet goodies inside if the north wind doth blow. After you've sampled the coffee latte and pastry or indulged in one of the many goodies in the deli case, it's time to browse among all the wonderful specialty foodstuffs cramming the shelves around the room. It always reminds me of what Alice must have seen as she fell slowly down the rabbit hole, seeing jars of marmalade and other delectables as she drifted past.

The Market has a fine selection of teas, from yerba maté and hibiscus through jasmine, oolong and gun powder to English and Irish breakfast. They also have coffee beans and chocolates, including truffles of various kinds. Crackers, especially the English water crackers, are well represented, as are many kinds of specialty pasta, olive oils and gourmet fattening dessert toppings.

Their deli case is as sophisticated as the rest of their offerings, with a nice range of cheeses like Stilton, Gouda, Jarlsberg, Crousin, (a semi-soft cheese with peppercorns) and a chicken liver mousse with truffles. Salads are a little more mundane, but tasty, and the hot case has beef, chicken and pasta selections.

The dessert case is full of sinful tortes and pastries, including Viennese torte and lemon or chocolate mousse. The sociable atmosphere and comfortable ambiance make The Market a pleasure.

Pete's Fruits & Vegetables

5606 E. Cedar 393-6247
Monday–Saturday, 7 am–7 pm; Sunday, 7 am–6 pm.

Pete's smells like an old-fashioned greengrocer's, with vegetables still redolent of the earth. All fresh and delicious-looking, his fruits, vegetables and fresh herbs are enticing, making healthy eating a pleasure. There's also a good selection of nuts, like fresh pistachios, raw cashews, piñon nuts and others. Pete has a range of specialty items, and, right next to the cash register, several delectable Greek desserts!

Wild Oats Market

2260 East Colfax 320-1664
12131 East Iliff, Aurora 695-8801
Daily, 8 am – 10 pm.

I'm more familiar with the Denver store, which is on the corner of Colfax and York. It's smaller than the Aurora store, but they have the same kinds of items at both stores. Their produce is often organic, and includes some unusual items like tomatillos and bok choy. They have bulk spices, including Sichuan peppers, which I hunted for in vain, and finally almost gave up and bought rose-colored peppers instead! However, here they have the real thing, and the peppers are quite wonderful, aromatic and delicious.

Here you'll find bulk lentils, beans and peas, as well as many kinds of flour, including millet, lots of specialty grains, and more kinds of granola than I've ever seen together in one place.

Many kinds of bread are available here, and miso, tofu, kefir, many different kinds of yoghurt, organic baby food and great dried fruit snacks like dried kiwi (delicious!), and dried mangoes and papaya spears.

Although the emphasis is on natural foods, they also have a good number of gourmet items, like Chocolate Ecstasy gourmet fudge topping, the Guiltless Gourmet line of fat-free dips, such as cheddar queso and mild black bean dip. They also carry some good crackers, like Carr's English Water Biscuits, as well as matzoh and lavosh.

Visit Wild Oats for hard-to-find gourmet and ethnic items, as well as bulk spices and natural foods.

Heavenly Ice Cream

No-one knows who invented ice cream. However, it is known that the Roman Emperor Nero sent regularly to the mountains for snow, to be served flavored with honey and fruit. Then there's a lull of about a thousand years in the history of ice cream, until at the close of the thirteenth century Marco Polo returned to Italy from the East with a recipe for a frozen dessert made with milk. This probably evolved into ice cream in Italy, and was brought to France by Catherine de Medici when she married the man who eventually became Henri II.

Ice cream was much loved by Charles I of England before his unfortunate demise at the hands of the Roundheads during the English Civil War. His son, James II, indulged in ice cream often, and there is an entry in his household accounts for a dozen dishes of the cold, sweet stuff in 1686. The first recipe for ice cream appeared in France around 1700, and there were many such recipes in British cookbooks during the eighteenth century.

So far this "food fit for the gods", as it was described in one treatise, was available only to the aristocracy. That changed in 1670, with the opening of Cafe Procope in Paris, where ice cream and sherbet were available for sale. From then on, it became common for Parisian cafes to sell their own ice cream specialties.

Although the Romans may have invented ice cream, it took Americans to popularize it. In 1777, one Philip Lenzi took out an ad in the New York Gazette advertising the daily availability of his ice cream. When Brillat-Savarin, the French gourmet, returned to France from a trip to New York, he wrote that French immigrants to the U.S. were making their fortunes selling ice cream to the masses.

Ice cream was still only within reach of the wealthy, but as ice houses became more common, in the early nineteenth century, ice cream became available in ice cream parlors in major cities. In 1846, the hand-cranked ice cream maker was invented. By 1850, this had brought ice cream into the realm of the necessities of life. At the beginning of the twentieth century, technical developments made full-scale manufacture of ice cream possible. By the 1920's, ice cream had become the favorite food of the typical American, and except for a slight dip in popularity after the repeal of Prohibition, it's never looked back.

Soda fountains and ice cream parlors became the place to go after the movies, and they were glamorized in the movie business by starlets who were discovered at Schwab's drugstore in Hollywood. During World War II, ice cream became the symbol of American morale. During the 1950's, the trend towards air-filled inferior ice cream began, and gourmet ice creams began to spring up around the country to counteract this trend.

Today, ice cream is as varied in flavor and consistency as good wine. Hundreds of flavors are available, and ice cream, frozen yoghurt and even non-dairy substitutes can be found everywhere.

All for the Better

3501 S. Clarkson, Englewood 781-0230
Monday–Saturday, 11 am–9 pm; Sunday, 2–9 pm.
Winter hours: Closed Sunday.

This little white-painted brick building with its striped awning is like an old-fashioned ice cream parlor, right across the street from Swedish Hospital. It's a cute, friendly place with lots of light, lots of space between tables–and an enormous yak's head on the wall in the back room!

They have sodas, floats, malts and sundaes as well as a good variety of homemade ice cream, including oreo cookie, blueberry cheesecake, coffee, chocolate chip mint, pineapple sorbet and the usual vanilla, strawberry and chocolate. They have ten foot banana splits too, just in case you want to surprise an ice cream-loving friend for a birthday or anniversary!

One of the nice things about this place is that they give you a cardboard cone with your ice cream cone, so if it gets drippy, your clothes survive. A nice touch, I think. Soups and sandwiches are available as well as ice cream. Now, if only someone could tell me the story of that yak...

Bonnie Brae Ice Cream

799 S. University 777-0808
Monday–Friday, 10 am–10 pm; Saturday & Sunday, 8 am–10 pm.

Chocoholics, take note! If you're looking for Snickers Delight or Triple Death Chocolate, Bonnie Brae Ice Cream is for you! They have other delightful flavors, too, like lemon custard, amaretto peach, deep dish apple pie, and caramel custard. Their strawberry icecream has real strawberries in it instead of mere strawberry syrup!

Judy Simon, owner of Bonnie Brae Ice Cream, grew up in Virginia churning ice cream for friends and family, according to local legend. Her ice cream was so good that they all urged her to produce it commercially. She complied (probably so they wouldn't keep bugging her to hand-churn the delicious stuff for them!) and in the summer of 1986, Bonnie Brae Ice Cream was born. Judy takes care with her ice cream. Her Grand Marnier chocolate chip has real Grand Marnier in it. Her vanilla ice cream is made with 100% pure vanilla. The store serves floats and malts as well as ice cream.

In case you don't like ice cream at all, this ice cream parlor also has muffins, like lemon poppy seed, and ginger with cream cheese, and lemon bars, lemon ginger snaps and other goodies. They also have a fresh lemon fizz drink that sounds refreshing for a warm summer day. This is a nice, old-fashioned style ice cream parlor–the kind of place to take the kids for dessert on a summer evening.

Ice Cream Makers

1207 E. 9th Avenue (9th & Corona) 831-4010
Monday–Friday, 11 am–11 pm, Saturday 9 am–11 pm.
Sunday 9 am–10 pm.

If you're old enough to know what White House flavor ice cream is, you've been around the block a time or two. That's what David Green, who owns the Ice Cream Makers with Robert Brann, told me, anyway. "The senior citizens always recognize the flavor right away," he said. It's a vanilla based ice cream, with cherries and nuts. Tonya, who works for David, agrees. When asked what

exactly was in it, she replied, "I always tell them it's full of fruits and nuts, just like the real White House."

David learned to make ice cream from a fellow called Roger who owns one of the stores at Stapleton Airport called Roger's Top Cone. According to David, Roger's store was once featured in Time Magazine and voted one of the best ice cream stores in the country.

There's been an ice cream store at this location for at least twenty years, so perhaps that's why the seniors remember their flavors so well! David has invented some new flavors as well–Mississippi Mud is one. He's had a lot of support from his customers, who ask him to make different kinds of ice cream for them. He's made orange custard chocolate chip, cappuccino oreo, and even avocado blackberry swirl, which he says was surprisingly good.

This is the only place I've seen with a chocolate chip cookie cone, which has become very popular over the summer. They also have a new espresso machine, which can deliver lightning-quick coffee drinks. Might be good for those fruits and nuts at the White House!

Lickety Split Icecream

2039 E. 3th Avenue 321-1492
Daily, 11 am – 11 pm.

Lickety Split has a large selection of homemade ice cream flavors, some of which are available in a number of other places – restaurants and coffee shops – as well as in its own location in Capitol Hill. They have all kinds of soda fountain drinks, malts, and specials like the Piggy Split, which is 7 scoops of icecream, 2 bananas, toppings, whipped cream and jimmies. They have New York egg creams, coffee and cappuccino and a large variety of icecream,

including my very favorite, ginger, made with candied ginger and absolutely yummy.

They have the usual choices of cones and dishes and, of course, they make special occasion cakes and decorate them to your specifications. There's a book of ideas on the counter.

There are tables and chairs outside and inside, so you can sit around and enjoy the many different ice cream delights Lickety Split has to offer.

Magill's World of Ice Cream

8016 W. Jewell, Lakewood 986-9968
Monday – Saturday, 9 am – 10 pm; Sunday, 11 am – 10 pm.

This ice cream parlor has been in business for fourteen years, making 30-odd flavors of icecream fresh for its customers, including watermelon sherbet, ice cream sandwiches, mini-sundaes, snowballs, and O'Clairs that look like eclairs but are made of ice cream. They also make their own ice cream cakes, ranging from a sentimental heart-shaped cake with delicate icing

in two shades of pink to a cake with a toilet on it in icing and the caption, "Another year down the drain".

Their ice cream pies, like turtle, French silk, mud pie and grasshopper, look delicious. Their soft-serve ice cream is real ice cream, not ice milk. It's obviously a fixture in Lakewood, so if you're in the neighborhood, this is the place for an ice cream fix..

Soda Rock Fountain

2217 E. Mississippi 777-0414
Daily, 11:30 am–4:30 pm, & 6:30 pm–9 pm.

Ice cream sodas, shakes, malts and egg creams at an old-fashioned soda fountain with a marble-topped counter and those little juke box things at the tables–Soda Rock fountain is really a fun place to visit. It's a classic soda fountain right out of the 50's, reminding us of James Dean, cherry cokes, and first romances. They also have smart drinks and gatorade for the health-conscious, or those fresh from a run or walk in nearby

Washington Park.

Jayjanna Oliver has been the owner and chief ice cream scooper here for the past three years, though the soda fountain has been here at least 11 years, she says. She's added gourmet coffee drinks, and they serve burgers and hot dogs as well. In addition to the usual flavors, they have smurf flavor, which tastes rather like fruit loops, according to Jayjanna. For a real nostalgia rush, Soda Rock Fountain is the place!

Presidential Food Facts

Thomas Jefferson introduced ice cream, macaroni and waffles to the U.S. He loved to cook, and wrote an essay called, "Observations on Soup".

How Sweet It Is...

Chocolate is one of the most luxurious and decadent foods in the world. It originated in the Americas, and was taken back to Europe by the Spanish conquistadors. The Europeans refined and changed it from a drink to a seductive and delicious confection. It was considered so morally dangerous that at one time eating chocolate in church was a sin!

It's believed that cacao trees, the source of chocolate, grew wild in the Amazon valley more than 4,000 years ago. The Mayans were supposedly the first to cultivate the cacao tree and introduced it to the Yucatan in Mexico in the seventh century A.D. Both the Mayans and the Aztecs thought the cacao beans were a gift from the gods, and used them for ceremonial functions and also as currency. The beans were used to make a drink highly prized by Moctezuma, who drank it before entering his harem. This chocolate drink, called "chocolatl" by the Aztecs, was given to good fighters but not to those who were cowardly.

Cortez brought the secret of making the highly spiced chocolatl back to Spain, where Spanish monks altered it by adding sugar and vanilla. This sweet, delicious drink became a favorite of Spanish aristocrats. Anne of Austria may have been the first chocoholic. She brought the drink with her when she married Louis XII of France. It was all the rage at Versailles.

Coenraad van Houten, a Dutchman, invented a cocoa press in 1828. It made chocolate more palatable, so that it could be eaten as a confection, instead of just used as a drink.

Rodolphe Lindt invented a way of kneading chocolate called "conching" which made the texture smooth instead of grainy. The first eating chocolate was introduced in England in 1847, and the first American candy bar was produced in 1894.

Chocolate Shops

Accent on Chocolate

1596 S. Pearl 778-9188
Summer hours: Tuesday–Saturday, 11 am–5 pm.
Closed Sunday & Monday.
Winter hours: Daily, 10 am–9 pm.

"Promise me anything–but buy me chocolate," says the sign on the door of this cute little shop on South Pearl Street. Inside, there are boxed novelties like chocolate skis, boots and tennis racquets. There are also chocolate ties for Father's Day and T shirts that say things like, "Life begins with chocolate". Bonnie Newman, the owner, makes the chocolates herself, all the mint and raspberry creams, lollipops and many other lovely chocolate items. I liked the chocolate cameos and the boxes filled with leaves, all made of chocolate, colored chocolate brown and purple.

There are also fun chocolate popsicles, shaped like hearts or dinosaurs, and chocolate fudge squares. This is a friendly likeable neighborhood place, with an owner who's on the premises, working.

Blume's Chocolates

6911 S. University, Littleton 795-2506
Monday–Friday, 10 am–9 pm; Saturday, 10 am–6 pm;
Sunday, 11 am–5 pm.

This chocolate and candy store in the Southglenn Mall has been owned by Mary Carol Gleason and her family for over thirteen years, ever since they bought the local outlet of Blum's of San Francisco. Many of the chocolates are hand-dipped and there are some specialties I haven't often seen elsewhere, like dark chocolate covered orange peel. Their fudge and caramel apples are always popular, and they have many different kinds of chocolates, like pralines, peanut truffles, and orange sherbet creams.

For those who are looking for sugarless, they have sixteen kinds of sugar-free chocolates. There's also an outlet store at 2560 W. Main in Littleton, called Chocolates by Mary Carol, where you can buy Blume's chocolates at a discount. "We don't have all the frills over here, though," says Mary Carol.

Cardworks

3302 Youngfield, 232-9201
Monday–Friday, 9 am–6 pm; Saturday, 9 am–6 pm;
Sunday, noon–5 pm.

Nancy Becker's father and uncle encouraged her to open a store. One recommended a candy store and the other a greeting card store. Perhaps that's why Cardworks turned out to be a combination card, gift and old-fashioned candy store. It's located in a shopping center in Applewood, right off I-70 at Youngfield. Nancy carries a selection of chocolates from Hammond's in Denver, Patsy's in Colorado Springs and from other U.S. chocolate makers as far away as Vermont. At Christmas she often has European candies from Belgium, Switzerland, Holland and Germany.

The candy jars lining the counter are filled with such children's delights as gummy bears, sour apples, hard candy, licorice pontefract cakes (did you know that Pontefract is a coal mining town in the north of England?) They also have something I haven't seen anywhere else–double salted Dutch licorice–delicious–not too sweet but very flavorful. I also noticed that after I'd eaten it, I didn't want anything sweet (perhaps it was the salt?). So I'm hoping I've discovered a new dieting aid!

The beauty of this store is that you can buy candy or chocolate, have it beautifully wrapped, get a nice card to go with it and voila!–instant celebration.

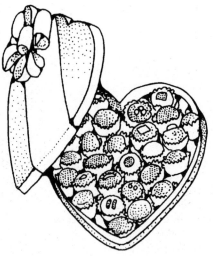

Chocolate Foundry

2625 E. Third Avenue 388-7800
Monday–Friday, 10 am–7:30 pm;
Saturday & Sunday, 10:30 am–6 pm.

This Cherry Creek chocolaterie specializes in chocolate molds, of which they have many. They also have dipped strawberries in season, and many different kinds of fudge. Owner and chocolatier Marilyn Nevison always makes something special and arresting in chocolate as a decor centerpiece for the store. When I was there, a gigantic ant and grasshopper celebrated the onset of summer, a reminder of Aesop's fable about the ant who worked all summer and put away stores for the winter and the grasshopper who had a good time but had no food for the cold weather. This won't happen to us if we shop at the Chocolate Foundry. We could probably put on enough weight to keep us going through the long winter with next-to-no food!

The Chocolate Foundry also has a specialty coffee bar, with espressos, cappuccinos and all those good drinks that go so delightfully with chocolate. For Christmas they make fudge mountains and they also have topographical maps in chocolate of Aspen, Steamboat, Crested Butte and other famous ski areas.

HOW CHOCOLATE IS MADE

Chocolate seeds, from the cacoa tree, differ according to the country and even the plantation where they are grown. Often chocolate manufacturers blend several varieties of seed. At the factory, beans are cleaned, weighed and roasted. Then the cocoa seeds are shelled, leaving the meat, called "nibs". The nibs are about 50% cocoa butter. The nibs are conched–crushed for a smooth texture. Cocoa butter is extracted and returned at the end of the process. The dark paste left after the butter is extracted is called chocolate "liquor". Confection made from the plain, hardened liquor is unsweetened chocolate. Sweet chocolate is made by adding cocoa butter and sugar before the liquor hardens. Milk chocolate is made by adding milk solids to the sweet chocolate formula. White chocolate is made from pure cocoa butter, milk, sugar and vanilla. Because it does not contain chocolate liquor, white chocolate is not true chocolate.

Dietrich's Chocolate & Espresso

1734 East Evans 777-3358 Fax: 623-8203
Sunday–Tuesday, 10 am–6 pm; Wednesday & Thursday, 10 am–9 pm;
Friday & Saturday, 10am–10 pm.Closed Sunday in summer.

Eric Dietrich is a man who definitely knows about chocolate. He's been in the chocolate business for 25 years, starting with an apprenticeship in Germany and continuing in Wisconsin, coming to Denver around 1977. He had a store on East Colfax for many years and is now located in the D.U. area. Eric has seen a lot of changes in people's tastes in chocolate over the years. He remembers in the 70's creams, caramels and nougats were more popular, whereas now he sees truffles as becoming more in vogue.

He's just started making his own line of truffles, of which the first two flavors are espresso and Grand Marnier. The next one will be a hazelnut flavor. They're simply delicious and go wonderfully with coffee. Eric also serves coffee in his store and has espresso, lattes and other specialty coffee drinks. His chocolates are simply beautiful, and he has many loyal customers who refuse to buy anywhere else. He also has some imported hard candies, like clear mints from Belgium and blackcurrant and raspberry filled éclairs from England. This is a lovely little store with a gorgeous selection of chocolates. I think you'll like it.

Divine Temptations

5820 Ogden 296-8212
Tuesday–Friday, lunch 10 am–2 pm, or call anytime to order.

If you ever need catering or chocolates and would like a manicure or facial at the same time, call Tammy Davis. Tammy has what I'd call a varied career: she makes chocolates in the season (fall, for Christmas, through Mother's Day), and she also does catering of all kinds, specializing in German and Italian food, makes special occasion cakes, like birthday and wedding cakes, and Mondays and Saturdays she works at a beauty salon. Divine Temptations is also open for lunch Tuesday–Friday 10–2, (just to make sure Tammy stays busy!) where she offers 3 or 4 lunch specials every day, and desserts.

Mmm, those desserts. Tammy uses lots of butter and cream, and has a special cake that's much sought-after by those in the know. It's a white chocolate cake with a dark chocolate mousse and raspberry purée filling. Her chocolates are all hand-made, with no preservatives, and she makes mints for weddings and other important events as well. So you can see why she calls her company Divine Temptations. Dinners for 2 (the romantic kind) to dinners for 250, Tammy can handle them, and she can make just about any kind of food you like. She won't do larger parties because she's afraid the quality would suffer–not to mention her sanity, is my belief! She's also such a pleasure to talk to and work with that you should really consider her for catering, chocolates or even a manicure!

Enstrom Candies

201 University (2nd & University) 322-1005
Monday–Saturday, 9 am–6 pm. Closed Sunday.

Enstrom's is a local chocolate maker, with their main factory in Grand Junction. They've been serving Denver since the 1950's and their small but lovely store in Cherry Creek is a pleasure to visit. Their almond toffee is legendary, and they also have truffles, dipped pretzels, lots of creams, and nuts like dipped almonds, cashews, pecans and macadamias.

The most unusual thing I saw was bulls' eyes, which apparently are marshmallows wrapped with caramel. They also had chocolate-covered gummi bears, which I haven't seen elsewhere. There are jelly beans and candies and lots of cups, pretty bags and boxes, to pack up your chocolates and candies in. Like many of the chocolate shops these days, they have no-sugar chocolates but beware! they're not non-caloric. But for diabetics or those who are trying to limit their sugar intake, they're great.

Godiva Chocolatier

3000 E. First Avenue (Cherry Creek Shopping Center) 321-0401
Monday–Friday, 10 am–9 pm; Saturday, 11 am–7 pm.
Sunday, noon–6 pm.

This is the place to buy chocolates for people you want to impress. Inside, on the counter, there's a price list in Japanese, because apparently chocolate is very expensive in Japan, and Japanese visitors come here to buy gifts for their friends and families. Godiva does have a reputation for excellence, and the store reflects this. There are beautifully wrapped and boxed gift packages such as their cordial collection or the deluxe truffle assortment. There is also a selection of hand-dipped candied fruits like pineapple and orange rind.

Godiva Chocolates are made in Belgium and their labeling in the case is often in French as well as English. They have a selection of corporate gift options and also a charitable gift program that allows you to donate to one of three charities when you buy a certain gift package. There's even a line of Godiva gourmet coffees to go with your chocolates!

Godiva gives out a little leaflet about caring for your chocolate. Here are their tips, which they've kindly consented to share with us:

1. Chocolate should be stored away from sunlight, moisture, heat and strong odors.

2. Chocolate should be kept at room temperature for 2–3 weeks, refrigerated up to 3 months or frozen for up to 6 months.

3. When storing in refrigerator or freezer, seal chocolate inside two plastic bags.

4. Thaw chocolate 2 hours from refrigerator; 6 hours from freezer.

5. Chocolate tastes better when eaten at room temperature.

Hammond Candy Company

2550 W. 29th Avenue 455-2320
Monday–Friday, 8:30 am–5 pm; Saturday, 10 am–3 pm.
Closed Sunday.

Located just off Speer Boulevard and 29th Avenue, Hammond's has been in business 72 years. All the chocolates are made on-site, and range from creams and caramels to almond bark and their famous Rocky Mountain almond toffee. At holiday times, they make candy canes, peppermint pillows, satin straws, traditional ribbon candy and hand-made whirl suckers. They also sell mints, which are made fresh weekly, for weddings and other special events.

Specialty flavored popcorns, candy apples and nutty korn (made of nuts and fresh popcorn glazed with candy) are popular, as are their piggy backs–caramel with pecans, covered with milk chocolate.

Lydia's Inc.

7853 W. Jewell, Lakewood 989-5460
Monday–Friday, 9 am–5 pm. Closed Saturday & Sunday.

They were making chocolate roses at Lydia's when I walked in and there was a wonderful smell of cherries. Roses are what Lydia's is famous for, and they ship them to stores all over the country. They are really quite beautiful and perfect-looking, in delicate shades of pink, mauve, rose, apricot, peach, white...

Lydia's also has many other chocolates–the usual flavors, plus some less usual flavors like raspberry truffles, orange jellies, champagne truffles clothed in white chocolate, and coconut joy covered with milk chocolate. There are pretty baskets and cute tins to put the chocolates into and teddy bears to send with the chocolates, so they make a complete gift package. But the roses are what Lydia's is really famous for, and they'll wrap and ship them for you too.

Miz G's Confectionary

2001 Youngfield, Unit G 239-6784
Monday–Thursday, 11 am–8 pm; Friday & Saturday, 11 am–9 pm.
Closed Sunday.

Mary and John Garin run this little chocolate, candy and lunch place in Applewood. John makes pies and cheesecakes for special orders, and their chocolates are specially made for the store. They have chocolate boxes (that is, boxes made of chocolate) filled with candy, as well as a variety of truffles, orange and raspberry sticks, a selection of different chocolate centers and specialty items, like chocolate rosebuds covered with bright, shiny foil. They carry yoghurt and Lickety Split ice cream.

John makes his own cookies, including chocolate chip, oatmeal raisin, peanut butter, cinnamon and sugar, and sugar cookies. Their lunch prices are reasonable and the shop is clean and pretty.

Rocky Mountain Chocolate Factory

1512 Larimer 623-1887
Monday & Tuesday, 10 am–9 pm; Wednesday & Thursday, 10 am–
10 pm; Friday & Saturday, 10 am–11 pm; Sunday, 11 am–9 pm.
Also at
7200 W. Alameda, Lakewood 936-8004
Aurora Mall, Aurora 366-4000
8501 W. Bowles, Littleton, 972-0186
Cinderella City, 781-0229.

Rocky Mountain Chocolate Factory is a Colorado franchise with a factory in Durango that supplies all the stores. I visited the one in Writer Square, owned by Don Marsh. Outside, in the summer, an enormous teddy bear sits, ready to have his picture taken with enterprising tourists. And inside, what an attractive place it is, with a tray of hand-dipped strawberries sitting on the counter as you walk in and cases filled with delectable chocolate goodies, like huge chocolate-covered caramels, including raspberry and seafoam, chocolate-covered toffee, boxes of 8 gourmet truffles, fruits like dipped apricots and a whole slew of fudges, like chocolate peanut butter, cappuccino, chocolate pecan and German chocolate.

Most intriguing is the aspen cream. I wonder what it could

possibly be? The most expensive cream ever invented? Essence of movie star? Turns out it's just a maple and brown sugar mixture. Perhaps we should invent a story and start a legend. Don Marsh is most obliging, and gives me a potted history of the company, from its start in Durango 12 years ago to more than 100 stores nationwide today! They dip their own

strawberries, as well as chocolate-covered apples and caramel apples, and also raspberries in season! Their fudge is made fresh in the store as well. Their bears are what other chocolateries call turtles, and come in many flavors: peanut, macadamia and almond, to name a few.

As I am about to leave, a frantic woman comes in and yells, "B-52's!" I'm ready to duck or dance, but it turns out she's referring to a kind of chocolate in the case that she's been searching for throughout the town. They're truffles, with kahlua and amaretto. They sound simply divine.

Russell Stover Candies

3333 Moline, Aurora 343-9383
Monday–Saturday, 9 am–5:30 pm; Sunday, noon–5:30 pm.

This is the place to go to find boxes of one particular kind of chocolate, if you're addicted to strawberry creams or maple creams or raspberry parfaits. However, more often than not they're not boxed for retail sale, so don't go to buy a gift for someone you want to impress! There are bargains to be had here, however, especially out of season. For example, chocolate Easter bunnies are selling in July for a fraction of their usual cost, and a summer candy bonanza includes a special on fudge and on Russell Stover's popular one pound assortment.

Summer is a slow time for the chocolate business, which really booms between October and Easter.

There is also a small selection of lemon squares, mint squares and other bulk candy. You can buy here in bulk and save a few bucks. Russell Stover has been in business since 1923, and you can still find their chocolates in many gift stores in Denver, even though their retail store on East Colfax is now closed. The outlet store is a little difficult to find, but can be reached by taking Peoria to 33rd and then driving west to Moline.

See's Candies

875 S. Colorado Boulevard 733-1854
Monday–Saturday, 9 am–6 pm. Closed Sunday.

Across the parking lot from Healthy Habits restaurant, this See's Candies store has a sign on the door that says, "A Happy Habit". The store looks brand new and elegant in black and white, with beautiful displays of different chocolate assortments, boxes and novelty chocolate items.

The shop is spacious and welcoming, and filled with all kinds of candies and chocolates, pastel bonbons, truffles, peanut brittle bars, butterscotch, chocolates and toffees.

There are many kinds of cordials, creams, caramels and other filled chocolates available by the pound.

The story behind See's Candy is that Mary See opened her own neighborhood candy store in California when she was a 71 year old grandmother. This was more than 70 years ago. Now there are See's Candy stores throughout the West.

There are some wonderful old photographs that See's puts inside its candy boxes, with stories from See's history. My favorite is the picture of customers waiting in line during World War II when sugar was rationed and candy was in short supply. Customers lined up in front of the See's Candy Store in Sacramento. Each customer was allowed to buy one pound of candy. When supplies ran out, the doors were closed until the next day when a new supply of candy arrived. See's has quality chocolates and a huge assortment of different and decadent centers.

Stephany's Chocolates

Tabor Center, 16th & Lawrence 623-4900
Also in Cherry Creek Mall, 377-7754; Westminster Mall, 429-7993;
Buckingham Mall, 755-4211; 4969 Colorado Blvd, 355-1522
Tabor Hours: Monday–Friday, 10 am–9 pm; Saturday, 9 am–6 pm;
Sunday, noon–5 pm.

Stephany's has been making chocolates in Colorado for over twenty five years. Their most popular item is their Colorado Almond Toffee, closely followed by their Denver Mints. They carry Joseph Schmidt truffles and novelty items like chocolate cars, crayons and hand-made lollipops.

Stephany's has an unusually large choice of sugar-free chocolates, including their own sugar-free truffles. Their stores are all located in shopping malls, except for their kitchens on North Colorado Boulevard, where you can also go to buy chocolates, but only during regular business hours.

Sweet Expressions

1480 W. 104th Avenue, Northglenn 451-1178
Monday, Tuesday & Thursday, 10 am–5:30 pm; Wednesday, 10 am–3 pm;
Friday, 10 am–7 pm; Saturday, 10 am–3 pm. Closed Sunday.

Inge, who owns this delightful little gift and chocolate shop, is extremely talented. She makes chocolate houses, churches, and at Christmas even an entire chocolate village! Her chocolate baskets are beautiful and I am particularly impressed by a lovely chocolate swan filled with flowers–roses and daisies, all extremely graceful and elegant. She has gift baskets, boxes and ribbons, to make anything you might buy into a pretty present.

Inge began her career in chocolate in a little town near Bramstedfeld in the far north of Germany, helping her mother make desserts for the family.

She then did an apprenticeship at a creamery, but turned to other work when she became the wife of a Texas minister and came to the U.S. In 1984, she started creating chocolate novelties in her home and she now has close to 3,000 molds. Her ornaments and chocolate popsicles in the shape of Santas, angels and Christmas trees are particularly charming, and she puts together chocolate houses, sleighs, trees and other items to make unique chocolate village scenes for her customers.

She makes her own toffee, and all the fillings for her chocolates, and they taste as good as they look!

One More Cup of Coffee...

Its flavor changes according to variations in soil, moisture and climate. It w
first used medicinally and then later incorporated into religious rituals. An
wherever it was found, it inspired the kind of passion that prompted peopl
beg, borrow or steal to take some home with them. No, we're not talking a
fine wine. We're talking about coffee.

In contrast to its exotic beginnings in Ethiopia and the Middle East, in Am
coffee has always been the people's drink. It's always been relatively inexp
sive, and drunk by just about everyone, from teachers to tycoons. It got its
kick-off here after the Boston Tea Party, when patriotic Americans began
drinking it in earnest (before that, tea was more popular in the colonies!).
quest for a good cup of coffee was open to everyone, and everyone's opini
was just about equal.

Not any more. Now, instead of just asking for a plain cup of coffee, we mig
just as easily ask for a latte, an espresso or cappuccino. Gentrification has
reached us where we live–at our breakfast tables! The proliferation of cof
houses, from downtown to the suburbs,and particularly in Cherry Creek
North, the home of the upper crust, proves it. I've surveyed those I feel ar
most worth visiting, but there are more opening all the time, so this is har
an exhaustive study. See also Dietrich's, the French Confection, the Choc
Foundry, and Chateau de Patisserie, among others.

Caffé Arabica

2200 Kearney Street 333-2401
Monday–Thursday, 7 am–10 pm; Friday & Saturday, 7 am–11 pm.
Sunday, 8 am–6 pm.

Jan Vilkaitis lives in Mayfair, pretty close to the Park Hill neighborhood where she opened Caffé Arabica. "I just felt the need for a neighborhood place like this," she says. The care she's put into the place is evident all around. It's an attractive, spacious room, with a changing gallery of art on the walls, and huge windows so you can watch all the people coming for Saturday morning coffee, as they arrive, often with their dogs in tow.

The coffee they serve as lattes or cappuccinos or sell as coffee beans is Silver Canyon, which Jan chose after tasting many coffees from many local roasters, and finding what she considers simply the best. "I'm not just someone looking for a neighborhood coffee place, I'm also a coffee nut!" she explains. She's just as choosy about her pastries, buying some from Bobby Dazzler, some from Warren Paul's Grand Central Station (the cheesecakes, of course, among other things!) and some from Child's. Everyone has their specialty, and she just tries to get what she likes best.

The cafe serves steamers, hot milk flavored with Italian syrups, and Italian sodas, and, in summer, iced coffee drinks and Lickety Split ice cream. At lunch time, there's soup and sandwiches. And, perhaps best of all, there's a games section for kids and adults. Puzzles and games are just sitting there, waiting for anyone in need of a little light amusement to come by and get them down off the shelf. This is a very attractive little neighborhood place, with entertainment on weekends.

SPECIALTY COFFEE DRINKS

ESPRESSO *Fresh-brewed, very strong black coffee brewed using pressure to concentrate the flavor. It's a dark roast with a slightly burnt flavor.*

CAFFE LATTE *A fresh shot of espresso, combined with steamed milk*

CAFE AU LAIT *Generally, this is coffee as the French prefer it–half coffee and half milk.*

ESPRESSO MACCHIATO *Espresso with a spritz of milk foam*

ESPRESSO CON PANNA *Espresso topped with whipped cream*

CAPPUCCINO *Approximately 1/3 espresso, 1/3 steamed milk, and 1/3 foamed milk*

STEAMER *Steamed milk with an Italian flavored syrup (almond, vanilla, and hazelnut are some of the most popular flavors)*

These drinks, with variations, can be enjoyed at any of the coffee houses in this section, and cappuccino and espresso are available in some restaurants around town as well. Starbucks and Java Hut come here from Seattle, the coffee capital of America, where coffee has become so much the rage that there's not only an espresso cart on every corner, but even a magazine devoted entirely to coffee and car washes with their own espresso machines! Other coffee houses, like the neighborhood places, or like Paris on the Platte, which has been here for several years, are home-grown.

Boyer Coffee Company

747 S. Colorado Boulevard (Belcaro Shopping Center) 289-3345
Monday–Friday, 7 am–6 pm; Saturday, 8 am–6 pm. Closed Sunday.
6820 S. University Boulevard 289-3345 (Hours same as above)
7295 N. Washington 289-3345 Monday–Friday, 7 am–5:30 pm;
Saturday, 8 am–2 pm.Closed Sunday.

Boyer's new coffee emporium at Belcaro is an attractive blend of wood and high tech, with coffee sacks adorning the walls. The coffee bar is secondary to the enormous counter housing a huge variety of coffees sold by the pound–over 125 different kinds. As well as a large selection of flavored coffees, Boyer's also has the least expensive coffee, starting at around $2 a pound for preground light Columbian. They also sell teas and spices. Their spices are mostly available in large quantities, and they have some unusual ones like juniper berries.

Brio

5 downtown locations open weekdays only
Arapahoe & 16th 534-8752 Monday–Friday, 6 am–4 pm.
110 l6th 620-9830 Monday–Friday, 6 am–5:30 pm.
730 17th 620-9828 Monday–Friday, 6 am–4 pm.
1225 17th 296-0260 Monday–Friday, 6 am–3:30 pm.
999 18th 297-3451 Monday–Friday, 6 am–2:30 pm.

These beautifully stylish, high-tech Italian-style coffee places are a treat for the eyes. They're exquisitely designed, with tile floors, sweeping counters and attractive fixtures. The Brio in the Equitable Building is twice as big as the others, and even has some banquette seating. Two of the Brio coffee bars serve sandwich lunches as well as pastries and bagels (Equitable Building and Prudential Plaza). Coffee by the pound varies in price from $7.75 to $12.00 per pound. The bean coffees for sale are listed in three categories: Varietals (by place, such as Columbian, Kenyan, etc.), Blends (Della Sera, Viennese) and Dark Roast (Espresso, French Roast). They also offer a selection of artsy coffee mugs.

Coffee West

201 Milwaukee 321-3138
Monday–Thursday, 6 am–9 pm; Friday, 6 am–10 pm;
Saturday, 7 am–10 pm; Sunday, 8 am–6 pm.

This small but upscale and friendly coffeehouse is beautifully decorated, with a romantic atmosphere and very attractive surroundings. During the summer you can also sit outside on the sidewalk and watch the upscale shoppers go by! Coffee West serves Torrefazione coffee. They also sell it by the pound. Each roast is named after a city in Italy. Their coffee is very mellow and is characterized as light, medium or dark roast, with one decaffeinated roast. All their coffee beans are priced under $10 a pound. Coffee West serves pastries and slices of cake as well as all kinds of gourmet coffee drinks and, in summer, granita (a kind of coffee ice made with espresso, sugar and milk that's the best summer drink ever invented), tea, mineral waters, lemonade, orange juice and Italian sodas.

Colorado Espresso Company

2075 S. University 744-2531
Monday–Thursday, 6:30 am–10 pm; Friday, 6:30 am–11 pm;
Saturday, 7:30 am–11 pm; Sunday, 8 am–6 pm.

After Debi Joens drove around Denver for two hours looking for a skinny latte, she knew what her mission in life was going to be. "I remembered in Seattle there were about 48 places where I could get a skinny latte in a 2 block square area," she explains. A skinny latte is a latte made with skim milk. Now Debi can get one any time she wants, at her own coffee place near the corner of University and Evans in the DU area.

This coffee shop also has bagels, muffins, scones and brownies, as well as lattes, cappuccinos and two kinds of granita. Coffee granita is available, and the other flavor depends on the mood of the day. When I'm there it's creamsicle, and that's exactly what it tastes like! Sometimes it's cherry vanilla, and they're inventing new flavors all the time.

Debi, who's nothing if not inventive, has a Question of the Day on the counter. If you can answer the question, you get 10% off your drink. The Question when I'm there has to do with the Holy Grail: what vicious beast guarded the Holy Grail and what was the name of the first knight to face it? Hey,

that's two questions! Debi has ideas for other fun activities too. She's planning on having a coffee happy hour 4–6 pm during the school year. And she wants to set up a dart board. This is a great little coffee shop that's looking to stick around. They carry a brand of coffee called Seattle's Best Coffee.

Presidential Food Facts

At age 18, when he was a soldier in the Civil War, William McKinley drove a coffee wagon to the men on the battlefields.

Common Ground

3484 W. 32nd Avenue   458-5248
Monday–Thursday, 6:30 am–11 pm; Friday, 6:30 am–12 midnight;
Saturday, 8 am–midnight; Sunday, 8 am–11 pm.

This is another reminder of college hangouts from the past, a big barn of a room with wood floors, a friendly atmosphere with games and newspapers that encourage you to stay a while and talk, socialize and enjoy. They serve pastries as well as all kinds of coffees and other drinks, and create a comfortable family atmosphere.

This is a neighborhood coffee house, serving pastries and light lunches as well as lattes, espressos, cappuccinos and other coffee drinks. They also have Lickety Split ice cream. It's a pleasant place to sit and drink coffee, with huge windows, a few tables outside in the summer and an area of toys and games for children. They serve Silver Canyon coffee and also sell it by the pound.

Grounds for Coffee

7615 W.38th Avenue, #B 101, Wheat Ridge   423-3455
Monday–Saturday, 7 am–7 pm.

It's hard to believe that this bright little coffee shop is actually a franchise out of Salt Lake City. It has a nice family atmosphere, and caters to high schoolers in the morning and hospital employees from Lutheran and the surrounding medical buildings who visit during lunch.

They have coffee by the pound, ranging in price from $7-$15 per pound. They also sell a coffee extract or concentrate called Liquid Grounds that can be used for iced coffees and cappuccinos. You can get lattes or other specialty coffee drinks, and Italian sodas as well. There's a small selection of sandwiches and yoghurt for takeout.

Java Creek

287 Columbine (3rd & Columbine) 377-8902
Monday–Saturday, 7 am–10 pm; Sunday, 8 am–5 pm.

This warm and friendly little place has a relaxed and casual atmosphere that really invites you to stay and talk or read the magazines from the rack in the corner. Java Creek has a few coffees by the pound, including Cafe Amico. This coffee is special in that 30% of the profits go to a non-profit corporation dedicated to improving the quality of life for children and their families in coffee-growing communities. They also serve sandwiches and soups, a variety of teas, including "live" Chai (an Indian spiced tea), juices and Italian sodas.

Java Hut

6603-C Leetsdale Drive (Monaco & Leetsdale) 333-0655
Monday–Saturday, 6 am–9 pm; Sunday, 7 am–noon.

Part of the coffee deluge from Seattle, Java Hut carries coffee beans called Seattle's Best Coffee. They serve the usual gourmet coffee drinks, iced latte, cappuccino and Italian sodas in the summer, and they have a variety of edibles, including scones, cookies, croissants and biscotti.

Their coffee by the pound prices are reasonable, at about $7.65, and they have a wide variety of magazines for their customers to sit and read. There's also a fish tank, for those who want to simply sit and relax. This is not a fancy place, probably designed with the high school students across the way in mind, but it's a pleasant place to stop for a cup of coffee and a bite.

Latta's Espresso Company

300 East Sixth Avenue, #5 (6th & Grant) 733-1114
Monday–Thursday, 7 am–10 pm; Friday & Saturday, 7 am–midnight;
Sunday, 9 am–5 pm.

What an attractive little coffee shop this is, very close to downtown but with its own parking right in front. And the decor! Great furniture by Philippe Starck, the ritzy

French designer, all in rose, teal, black and grey, with wonderful high-tech European lighting and glass counters. They also serve and sell Torrefazione coffee, just like Coffee West in Cherry Creek. This is a smooth, mild coffee and of its blends Milano and Venezia are lighter, Napoli and Palermo are darker and Perugia and Roma are medium roasts.

For gourmet coffee drinks in an upscale and sophisticated atmosphere close to downtown, Latta's is hard to beat.

Old World Coffee & Tea Company

1512 Larimer Street, Writer Square 595-8285
Monday–Friday, 8 am–6 pm; Saturday, 10 am–6 pm;
Sunday, noon–5 pm. Open till 9 Thursdays in summer.

This is an adjunct to the Creative Cook, a gourmet kitchen store, and has an unusual variety of coffees from several different roasters, including Silver Canyon, Denver Coffee, Superior and First Colony. They also have a large range of teas, lots of lovely collectible teapots, as well as coffeepots and a lot of coffee mugs.

There's also a selection of herb teas and some nifty gift items like cowboy coffee and fartless popcorn (is there any other kind?) as well as some imported jams and jellies. The Creative Cook side of the store has cooking utensils, pots, pans etc. as well as gourmet items for the kitchen.

Paris on the Platte

1553 Platte Street 455-2451
Monday–Thursday, 11 am–1 am; Friday, 11 am–4 am;
Saturday, noon–4 am; Sunday, 7 am–1 am.

This is the only place that seems to encourage smoking. Maybe it attracts the smokers who feel unwelcome in all the other coffee houses! It has a college hangout feel: wood floors, mix-and-match chairs, a chess set on a table in the corner and people sitting around talking, reading and studying. There are 16 different specialty coffees on the menu, including New Orleans-style cappuccino and Cafe Fantasia, a confection of hot chocolate, steamed milk and espresso, poured over a fresh orange slice and topped with whipped cream and grated orange peel. Paris serves soups, sandwiches and pastries, and there's also a bookstore for your browsing pleasure!

MAKING A GOOD CUP OF COFFEE

Espresso and cappuccino machines can help you make some of the specialty coffees offered in these coffee houses at home. But if you're not looking to invest in a whole new coffee-making system, here are some tips for making good regular coffee:

1. Start with good beans. This usually means buying specialty beans and grinding your own rather than buying ground coffee.

2. Use fresh, cold water.

3. Make sure your coffee pot or coffee maker is clean. Oils and other substances from your coffee remain as residues on your equipment. Don't remove them with soap as it will leave a soap residue. Clean your coffee pot with a little baking soda.

4. Use the correct grind of coffee for your coffee maker, or medium grind for drip coffee.

5. Measure the coffee properly. The recommended amount of ground coffee per 6 oz. cup is 2 level tablespoons.

6. Serve your coffee fresh–once it's been left sitting on a hot plate the aromatics begin to evaporate. Experts recommend pouring freshly brewed coffee into a thermos or vacuum bottle to keep it both hot and fresh. (I just turn off the warmer on my coffee maker and reheat my coffee by the cup in the microwave.)

7. A percolator is not recommended for good coffee because it tends to boil the coffee and produce a bitter brew.

Store your coffee beans in an airtight container until you're ready to use them. Then grind only the amount you intend to use. Coffee beans can be stored in the freezer for up to 3 months without losing quality.

The Market

1445 Larimer 534-5140
Monday–Friday, 6:45 am–11 pm; Saturday, 8 am–midnight;
Sunday, 8 am–6 pm.

Long the place to see and be seen on weekend mornings downtown, this Denver institution has lost none of its charm. Sitting outside on a warm day, it seems that you'll probably see everyone you know strolling through Larimer Square if you only sit there long enough. Inside there's a specialty store and deli with the atmosphere of an old general store. You can sit and eat, people-watch or examine the selection of cookies, candies, vinegars, teas and other items that line the walls. They have the usual specialty coffee drinks and some good muffins and pastries. See also listing under Markets.

Peaberry Coffee Ltd.

3031 E. 2nd Avenue (2nd & St. Paul) 322-4111
Monday–Thursday, 6:30 am–10 pm;
Friday & Saturday, 6:30 am–11 pm; Sunday, 7 am–7 pm.
Also at: 1685 S. Colorado Boulevard 756-4111; 1201 16th St.
(Tabor Center) 595-4111; 5070 E. Arapahoe Road 388-4111

This is a very upscale, fun place with a coffee roaster in the middle of the floor. They have an enormous selection of coffees by the pound, priced from $6.45 for Columbian to $16.95 for Kona extra fancy. They have nine decaf coffees and a large number of flavored coffees. They even have four decaf flavored coffees! Their selection of coffee machines is extensive–from thermoses to espresso machines. In addition to coffee they also serve teas, Italian sodas, hot cider and eggnog in season and specialty drinks like eggnog cappuccino.

Starbucks

2701 East 3rd Avenue (3rd & Clayton) 331-9910
Monday–Saturday, 6:30 am–10 pm; Sunday, 7 am–7 pm.
Also at: 2nd & Fillmore 388-7565; Arapahoe & I-25 689-0728
6200 S. Syracuse Way, Greenwood Village 721-7611
Quebec & County Line Road 779-5221

These are the Starbucks stores open as we go to press, but they're springing up all over the city like mushrooms after rain. Hours are similar in all the stores, but often the suburban stores close earlier. Call individual coffee houses for the exact times they're open.

In addition to the usual gourmet coffee drinks like espressos, cappuccinos and lattes, Starbucks has such seasonal specialties as steamed cider and eggnog caffe latte, as well as hot chocolate, orange juice and mineral waters. They sell pastries, and coffee by the pound, as well as coffee mugs, espresso machines and other coffee paraphernalia.

STORE INDEX

INDEX BY STORE TYPE

BAKERIES

André's Confiserie Suisse, 25
Bagel Nook, The & Bagel Nook South, 16
Bagel Stop, 16
Bagel Store, 17
Bluepoint Bakery, 7
Bobby Dazzler, 7
Cakes by Karen, 8
Celestial Bakery, 13
Chateau de Patisserie, 21
Child's Pastry Garden & Child's Pastry Shop, 10
Danish Delight Bakery, 19
Das MeyerPastry Chalet, 26
Dave-Pan Bagel Bakery, 17
Dimmer's Home Bakery, 27
El Alamo, 30
Forever Bakery, 14
Fratelli's, 10
French Confection, 21
Gaspare's Bakery, 29
Great Harvest Bread Co., 11
Jacobs Bagelry, 18
Korean Rice Cake, 14
La Favorita, 30
La Patisserie Française, 22
La Petite Boulangerie, 22
Le Bakery Sensual, 37
Le Délice, 23
Mama Pirogi's & Other Peasantries, 20
Manna Bakery, 12
Mexidans, 31
New York Bagel Boys, 18
Omonia Bakery, 28
Panaderia Guadalajara, 32
Panaderia & Pasteleria Santa Fe, 34
Panaderia Rodriguez I & II, 33
Paris Bakery, 24
Pastaleria del Norte, 35
Rheinlander Bakery, 27
Rosales Mexican Bakery, 36
Sweet Soirée, 24
The Bagel Stop, 16
Vinh Xuong Bakery, 15
Vollmers Bakery, 12
Wheat Ridge Bakery & Creamery, 13
Warren Paul's Grand Central Station, 12
Wheat Ridge Dairy & Bakery, 13

DELICATESSENS

Alpine Sausage Co., 45
Bagel Deli, 57
Belfiore's Italian Sausage, 50
Bender's Brat Haus, 46
Carbone Italian Sausage, 50
Continental Deli, 46
Deli Italia, 51
East Coast Italian Deli, 39
East Side Kosher Deli, 58
European Delights, 47
Gold Star Sausage Co., 39
Helga's German Deli, 48
Karl's F.F. Delicatessen, 49
Lala's Gourmet Mexican Deli, 61
Lonorado's Italian Sausage Meat Deli, 52
Mariano's Italian Deli, 53
Mortensen's Gourmet, 40
New York Deli News, 58
Ol Fashioned Italian Deli, 53
Our Daily Bread, 41
Plaza Deli, 59
Roberto's Sausage, 54
Rockies Deli & Bakery, 41
Rosen's Deli, 60
S & K Deli, 42
Star Market & Catering, 43
Tignon's Deli, 44
Tony's Italian Sausage, 55

CHOCOLATE SHOPS

COFFEE SHOPS

RECIPE INDEX